T H E **G R I D**

T H E **G R I D**

Edited by Alexander Streitberger

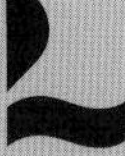

Lannoo

TABLE OF CONTENTS

FOREWORD

The Musée L is honoured to host this exhibition, which stems from a collaboration with Professor Alexander Streitberger (UCLouvain) on the subject of the grid, an emblematic structure in modern art that continues to inspire the imagination of contemporary artists.

Drawing on the Guillaume Wunsch and Monique Van Kerckhove collection, the exhibition focuses on major artworks from the 1960s and 1970s (geometric abstraction, Conceptual Art, Op Art, etc.), while also featuring a number of works by contemporary artists including Douglas Huebler, Sol LeWitt, François Morellet, Rosemarie Trockel, Vera Molnár, Christian Boltanski, Gina Pane and Esther Ferrer, to name but a few. The unexpected scope of the theme of the grid is illustrated in the essays and notes in this catalogue. In his introductory essay, Alexander Streitberger embarks us on a journey through time and space to reveal the complex and multiple roles that the grid played as a form, structure and device of artistic creation. Then, examining the grid as an icon of artistic modernity in countries outside the United States and Europe, Olivia Ardui turns to contemporary art in Brazil, a country that is represented in the exhibition through works by Claudia Andujar, Analívia Cordeiro and Anna Bella Geiger. Finally, the notices, which are structured around three main themes, cast a valuable light on the most important artworks in the exhibition.

We cannot emphasise it enough: teaching, researching, and serving society constitute the daily missions of the Museum L in its capacity of university museum. As the exhibition project unfolded, students were given the opportunity to engage with the artworks to participate in the exhibition design process, and to work on mediation by drafting notes on the pieces and artists presented. Such knowledge and skills transfer proved mutually enriching and fostered some wonderful collaborations.

We would like to express our warmest gratitude to Professor Alexander Streitberger, the exhibition's enthusiastic curator, and to his teaching assistant Olivia Ardui. We would also like to thank the students in the master seminar "History of Art from the Avant-Garde to Contemporary Art" for their contribution to this exhibition project. We should like to offer our appreciation to Anne Colla and Laurence Waterkeyn for their valuable work in coordinating the production of the exhibition and its catalogue.

Our heartfelt gratitude also extends to all the lending institutions and collectors who have shown their trust and accepted this collaboration. We should like to thank the Centre national des arts plastiques (CNAP) and the Espace de l'art concret, the Fonds régionaux d'art contemporain (FRAC) Franche-Comté, Grand Large (HDF), Lorraine, Normandie Caen, Occitanie Toulouse, the Fédération Wallonie-Bruxelles, the Musée des Arts contemporains de la Fédération Wallonie-Bruxelles (MAC's Grand-Hornu), the Musée de la Photographie de Charleroi, the Museum of Contemporary Art of Antwerp (M HKA), the Municipal Museum of Contemporary Art (SMAK), the ING Belgian Collection, the Vanmoerkerke Collection, the Philosophy Library of UCLouvain, the Library of the Université Saint-Louis Bruxelles, the KBR, the Wittert ULiège Museum, the Nadja Vilenne Gallery, the Anita Beckers Gallery, the Mendes Wood DM Gallery, Mr Piet Van Cauwenberghe, Mr Bernd Stiegler, Mr Guillaume Wunsch and Mrs Monique Van Kerckhove, and Mr Michael Ensdorf.

We are particularly grateful to our donors, Mr Wunsch and his wife Mrs Van Kerckhove. This exhibition could not have been staged without the presence of their collection.

And finally, I would like to conclude this preface with the words of Baudelaire, which Vera Molnár, the creator of the work on the cover, found so inspiring: "Monotony, symmetry, and surprise". Allow yourself to be captured by the grid as you explore the pages of this catalogue and the exhibition spaces.

Elisa de Jacquier de Rosée
Museum L Director a.i.

Alexander Streitberger

THE AMBIGUOUS GRID

A Journey Through the Meanders
of a Multidimensional Artistic Matrix

"Each grid has its own texture, uniqueness, individuating features, capacities for creative enactment, and relationship to other grids, as much as each person combines and utilizes a grid for him- or herself[1]."

Lattice, grating, mesh, network, screen, bars, matrix – all these words suggest what dictionaries call the "grid". Simultaneously terming a fence (the bars on the windows of a prison), a form of social, informational or economic distribution (the reading grid and the wage grid), an architectural or urban planning layout (the grid of a building plan), a means of map projection (the network of parallels and meridians), and a method of reproduction (Dürer's perspective machine and the screen or grid in photo-engraving), the grid is omnipresent in our daily lives, where it assumes a variety of functions and meanings. In *The Grid Book*, Hannah Higgins explores the history of the grid from the invention of the brick, circa 9000 BC, as a fundamental element of the wall as "a grid that is equal parts mortar and module", to grid computing as a virtual infrastructure that combines multiple computers to "coordinate complex and diverse information into a vast global knowledge network[2]".

Throughout the history of art, the grid is commonly associated with two historical moments: the emergence of abstract painting in Europe at the beginning of the twentieth century, with Piet Mondrian's neoplasticism at its pinnacle; and modernist and neo-avant-garde tendencies of the 1950s and 1960s, including

1   HIGGINS, Hannah B., *The Grid Book*, Cambridge, MA, MIT Press, 2009, p. 276.

2   *Ibid.*, p. 13 and p. 255.

Concrete Art, Minimal Art, Conceptual Art, Kinetic Art, and Optical Art. The discovery of the grid as a primary structure of artistic creation is directly related to a theoretical debate that took place in New York's artistic and intellectual scene in the 1970s in the wake of the exhibition *Grids Grids Grids Grids Grids Grids Grids Grids*, curated by Suzanne Delehanty at the University of Pennsylvania's Institute of Contemporary Art in 1972. In her introductory text for the catalogue "Top to Bottom, Left to Right", Lucy R. Lippard describes the grid as an emblematic principle of American and European art in the period from 1940 to 1970, which provides "an armature for a variety of styles, means and contents", or "an instrument by which to control the void [...] a way to violate the ominously blank surface.[3]" The artists exhibited included Carl Andre, Eva Hesse, Sol LeWitt, Agnes Martin, Robert Ryman, Ad Reinhardt and Andy Warhol, who, in the following years, would establish a canon of "grid artists" who were regularly featured in the art press, particularly in John Elderfield's and Amy Goldin's articles in *Artforum* magazine, respectively in May 1972 and September 1975[4]. Although there is no doubt that the grid has been in use in art since at least Ancient Egypt, its recognition as an autonomous artistic principle and its historiographical fortunes are directly connected to the discourse that took place in American art criticism in the 1970s. Rosalind Krauss's text "Grids" undoubtedly proved a major milestone in this discourse. Krauss begins her essay by chronicling the saga of modernist painting:

> "In the early part of this century there began to appear, first in France and then in Russia and in Holland, a structure that has remained emblematic of the modernist ambition within the visual arts ever since. Surfacing in pre-War cubist painting and subsequently becoming ever more stringent and manifest, the grid announces, among other things, modern art's will to silence, its hostility to literature, to narrative, to discourse[5]."

According to this Modernist interpretation, the structure of the grid, by virtue of its flatness, its geometric character, and its regular, antihierarchical arrangement, asserts the autonomy of art, while simultaneously opposing the mimetic and narrative principles of figurative art. But as we know (and Krauss was one of the first to point this out), this modernist fantasy of an autonomous, pure, and self-reflexive art conflicted with the utopian pretensions of avant-garde painters whose final aim was to reconcile the spiritual ambition of depicting the abstract mechanisms of the Universe with a scientific approach at the service of rational and technological progress[6]. Thus, Mondrian stated

3 Lippard, Lucy R., "Top to Bottom, Left to Right", in *Grids Grids Grids Grids Grids Grids Grids Grids*, cat., Institute of Contemporary Art, University of Pennsylvania, 1972, n.p.

4 Elderfield, John, "Grids", *Artforum*, May 1972, p. 52-59; Amy Goldin, "Patterns, Grids, and Painting", *Artforum*, September 1975, p. 50-54.

5 Krauss, Rosalind, "Grids", *October*, vol. 9, summer 1979, p. 50.

6 McNamara, Andrew, "Between Flux and Certitude: The Grid in Avant-garde Utopian Thought", *Art History*, Vol. 15, No. 1, March 1992, p. 61.

that the New Plastic aspired to geometric harmony, founded on "the *pure plastic of [abstract] relationships*", to express 'the universal, the harmony, the unity that are proper to the spirit[7]." Le Corbusier also believed that the rigorous grid of the Voisin plan, an urban planning project designed between 1922 and 1925 for the centre of Paris, epitomised the vision of a serial, mathematical and progressive order created to serve "a community without limits or hierarchy.[8]"

Far from being a pure, autonomous form, the grid is a complex, ambiguous structure that evokes the rational order of science while at the same time opening up hitherto unimagined spaces for imagination, intuition, and creativity. This ambiguity is further reinforced by the fact that "the slightest formal variation in the grid can produce, depending on the context, a complete transformation of meaning[9]." To appreciate the complexity and diversity of the grid in art, we shall look briefly at its age-old history as a tool of representation, before revisiting the debate raging in the 1970s and the paradoxes of the modernist grid. We will then examine the meanders of the ambiguous grid in art since the 1950s.

Projections of the World

As far back as the 18th Egyptian dynasty, i.e., between 1550 and 1292 B.C., wall painting was already executed using a preparatory drawing transferred to the wall by means of a grid that allowed the exact transfer of lines and colour planes[10]. The introduction and subsequent development of this transfer process was a direct result of the growing popularity of mimetic representation of reality through the rendering of space and volume. While in the 19th and 20th Dynasties paintings, two distinct grid systems were used to allow for the difference in size between standing kings and seated gods [Fig. 1], more recent examples seem to have abandoned this symbolic heterogeneity and adopted a homogeneous grid across the entire surface[11]. Yet the schematism of Egyptian wall paintings can be attributed to the fact that the grid was intended as an absolute, mechanically constructed system, adapted to the outlines of the body and limbs to the detriment of their organic forms. According to Erwin Panofsky, the Greeks inverted the relationship between the grid and the body, by starting with the human body to then relate it to other bodies and incorporate it into a coherent whole[12]. But the Greeks – and then the Romans – conceived the representation

7 MONDRIAN, Piet, "Neo-Plasticism: The General Principle of Plastic Equivalence" (1921), in Charles Harrison & Paul Wood (ed.), *Art in Theory; 1900-2000. An Anthology of Changing Ideas*, Oxford, Blackwell, 2003, p. 291-292.

8 McNAMARA, Andrew, *op. cit.*, p. 66.

9 DE CHASSEY, Éric, "Beyond the Grid / Après la grille", in *Abstraction/ Abstractions : géométries provisoires*, cat., Musée d'Art moderne, Saint-Etienne, Éditions du Musée d'Art moderne, 1997, p. 12.

10 DYETT, Marleen, *Aus der Perspektive – Raster, Gitter, Netze: Betrachtungen zu einem Formelement der Kunst*, Wurzbourg, Königshausen und Neumann, 2014, p. 9.

11 ROBINS, Gay, "Composition and the Artist's Squared Grid", *Journal of the American Research Center in Egypt*, Vol. 28, 1991, p. 41-43.

12 PANOFSKY, Erwin, "Die Entwicklung der Proportionslehre als Abbild der Stilentwicklung", *Monatsheft für Kunstgeschichte*, 14, Vol. 2, 1921, p. 194.

Fig. 1

Temple of Sety I at Abydos, 19th dynasty, drawing by Gay Robins, "Composition and the Artist's Squared Grid", *Journal of the American Research Center in Egypt*, vol. 28, 1991, p. 52

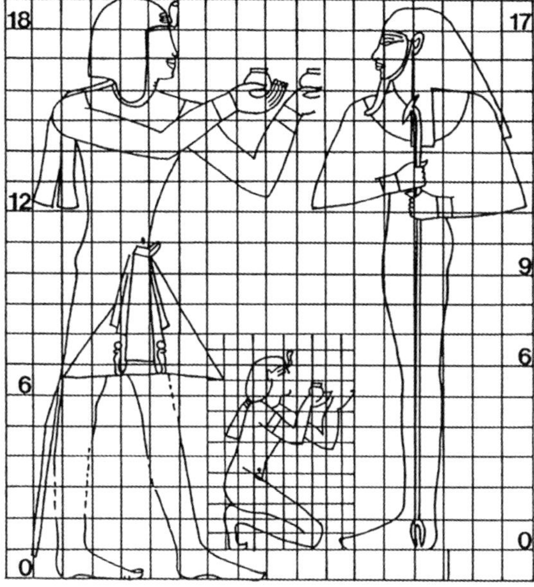

of space as a theatrical production – a "skenographia" – whose goal was not a systematic reconstruction of real space according to the laws of central perspective, but rather the creation of the illusion of a scenography[13].

In the Middle Ages, the function of the grid as a means to create the illusion of reality was supplanted by its symbolic status expressing vertical relationships between a material world (below) and a supernatural, divine reality (above). The vertical and horizontal lines in the illuminated text columns and miniatures of the late Middle Ages served to create representational and symbolic relationships between various elements across the page. In contrast, during the Renaissance, the grid was "conceived of as a *field* comprised of points and axes possessing either neutral or numerical (quantitative) value[14]". Leon Battista Alberti's *velum* and Albrecht Dürer's perspective machine [Fig. 2] perfectly incarnate the desire to submit the world to a rational, calculated system of representation, which would find its ultimate manifestation in the notion of central perspective as a conical projection, allowing a three-dimensional space (and the objects contained within it) to be mapped onto a two-dimensional plane. In his book *De pictura*, Alberti suggests the use

13 Dyett, Marleen, *op. cit.*, p. 15 and p. 20. See also Hans Belting, *Florenz und Bagdad: eine westöstliche Geschichte des Blicks*, Paris, Munich, Beck 2008, p. 27.

14 Williamson, Jack H., "The Grid: History, Use, and Meaning", *Design Issues*, Vol. 3, No. 2, Autumn 1986, p. 15 and p. 18.

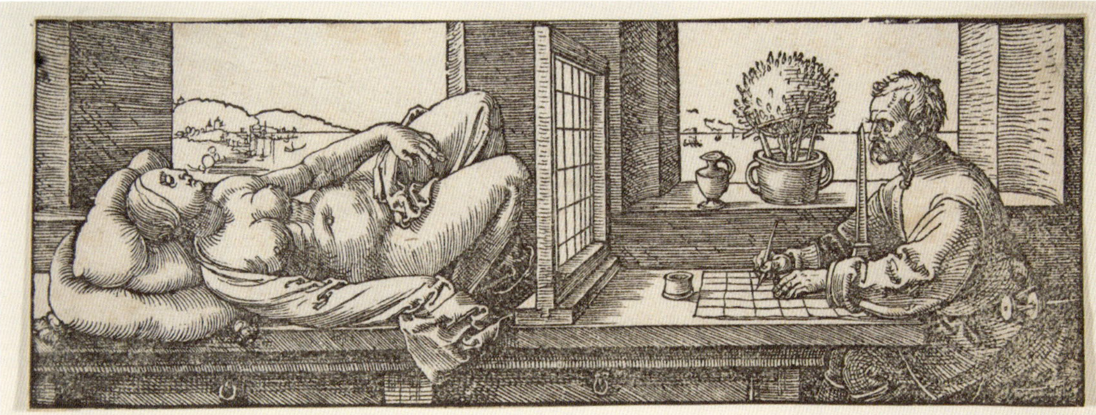

Fig. 2

Albrecht Dürer
*Draughtsman Making a Perspective Drawing
of a Reclining Woman.*

Books on Measurement
(a manual of measurement of lines, areas, and
solids by means of compass and ruler)
(third edition), Nuremberg, 1538

of an intersecting veil, positioned between the world and the eyes, for capturing the contours of things (*circumscriptione*) and assembling them in a composition (*compositio*). Here is Alberti's description of the process: "a veil loosely woven of fine thread, dyed whatever color you please, divided up by thicker threads into as many parallel square sections as you like, and stretched on a frame. I set this up between the eye and object to be represented, so that the visual pyramid passes through the loose weave of the veil[15]."

Published in 1538, Dürer's posthumous *Instruction on Measurement (Underweysung der Messung)* includes an engraving showing the functioning of the perspective machine, a device made up of a frame, the inside of which is squared by stretched strings. Using an eyepiece fixed to the end of a stick, the artist traces the shapes as seen through the grid onto a sheet of paper, also gridded, thus obtaining an exact copy of reality. The drawn rectangle, conceived by Alberti as a window opening onto the world, was transformed for good into a mechanical device enabling a faithful projection of reality onto the flat surface, which, according to Hubert Damisch, went "less in the direction of a rationalisation of vision than of a rationalisation of representation[16]". The vertical grid of the perspective machine is the equivalent of the projection of paving stones in perspective onto the canvas, as seen in many Renaissance paintings. The fact that the checkerboard motif was so popular in Renaissance painting[17] is partly due to the fact

15 ALBERTI, Leon Battista, *De pictura*, (*On Painting and On Sculpture. The Latin Texts of De Pictura and De Statua*), ed. by Cecil Grayson, London, Phaidon, 1972, p. 56-57.

16 DAMISCH, Hubert, *L'Origine de la perspective*, Paris, Flammarion, 1993, p. 49.

17 For example, Perugino's *Marriage of the Virgin*, dating from 1501-1504, or *The Ideal City of Urbino* (1476), the author of which is not certain.

that it helped to situate figures in space and to represent them correctly in perspective. Furthermore, Damisch points out that the two-colour chessboard "represents the simplest and most economical way of articulating, decorating and informing a surface[18]". The introduction of chess during the Renaissance as a "positional game, based on the opposition of two symmetrically conjugated fields" would turn it into a "stage" or "theatre" "where representation takes place", which would coincide with the emerging form of painting where the *istoria* assigns each figure its place ("*il suo luogo*")[19].

Thus, the construction of perspective and the depiction of a story are both based on the motif of a regular grid and its projection in space. In this way, the grid constitutes a principle of organisation and appropriation of the world through representation – but not just that! As several authors have pointed out, the invention of perspective as a means of dominating three-dimensional space chronologically coincides with Ptolemy's rediscovery, around 1400, of a method of cartographic representation whereby a grid of parallels and meridians shows places in terms of latitude and longitude[20]. By the mid-sixteenth century, Mercator's map projection used a grid to produce a precise projection of the globe on a flat map and became a valuable tool for navigating and colonising new territories. As with the mathematical perspective, Mercator's cartographic grid was designed to simulate and document spatial relationships on a flat surface, with the aim of measuring, controlling, and, ultimately, dominating the world[21].

Modernist Contradictions

Up until the 19th century, perspective dominated the representation of space in visual art. But while abstract painting steadily distanced itself from a mimetic rendering of things and embraced the emancipation of shapes and colours, it signalled a radical break with a pictorial technique designed to project the real world onto a flat surface. While Paul Cézanne noted that it was essential to learn to paint and "treat nature by means of the cylinder, the sphere, the cone" and that one could then "do everything that one pleases[22]", it became clear that geometry could no longer be envisaged as a mathematical method used to represent reality accurately, but rather, like a set of figures used to reveal the specific characteristics of painting. The grid is no longer used as an "intersection" between the world and the space of representation. Rosalind Krauss is unequivocal on

18 DAMISCH, Hubert, "L'échiquier et la forme 'tableau'", in Irving Lavin (dir.), *World Art: Theme of Unity in Diversity*, proceedings of the 26th international art history symposium, University Park, Pennsylvania, State University Press, vol. 1, 1989, p. 187.

19 *Ibid.*, p. 189-191

20 KISH, George, *La Carte. Image des civilisations*, Paris, Seuil, 1980, p. 38. For the relationship between perspective and cartography, see also Dyett, *op. cit.*, pp. 70-72.

21 WILLIAMSON, Jack H., *op. cit.*, p. 19.

22 CÉZANNE, Paul, "Lettre à Émile Bernard, 1904", in Émile Bernard, *Souvenirs sur Paul Cézanne et Lettres*, Paris, Société des Trente, 1921, p. 38.

this point: "But perspective studies are not really early instances of grids. Perspective was, after all, the science of the real, not the mode of withdrawal from it. [...] Unlike perspective, the grid does not map the space of a room or a landscape or a group of figures onto the surface of a painting. Indeed, if it maps anything, it maps the surface of the painting itself.[23]" On the basis of this observation, Krauss proposes a genealogy of the grid as a modernist structure, whose origins lie in European avant-garde painting, particularly with Cubism, De Stijl, Mondrian and Malevich. She continues by pointing out that, after the Second World War, the grid spread to the United States in the work of artists such as Ad Reinhardt, Agnes Martin, Robert Ryman and Sol LeWitt. As a planar, geometric spatial structure organised in an anti-hierarchical manner ("all-over"), the grid constitutes the ideal means of "crowding out the dimensions of the real and replacing them with the lateral spread of a single surface.[24]" If Krauss goes on to say that "The grid declares the space of art to be at once autonomous and autotelic", in that it refers only to its own creation, she is perfectly in line with Clement Greenberg's modernism, according to which every artistic discipline defines the limits and specificities of its medium to ensure its independence as a form of art[25].

In this perspective, the orthogonal grids that completely cover the paintings of American painter Agnes Martin merely reinforce the flatness of the surface to which they are applied: "The physical qualities of the surface, we could say, are mapped onto the aesthetic dimensions of the same surface[26]." However, this modernist approach presents a number of pitfalls. As we have already seen, Mondrian's and Malevich's non-figurative paintings do not merely refer to the inherent qualities of painting but seek a spiritual reality by suggesting a correlation between art and the cosmic order of the Universe. For her part, Agnes Martin adds an associative and sentimental dimension to her paintings when she evocatively titles her grid paintings (*Summer*, 1964; *The Sea, Ocean Water*, 1960; *Friendship*, 1963). This effect is further heightened by the colours and by the vibrations of the finely hand-drawn lines [Fig. 3]. In this, Krauss evokes the contradictory, paradoxical or schizophrenic nature of the modernist grid, which, whilst manifesting a materialist, logical and self-referential attitude, "provides us with a release into belief (or illusion, or fiction).[27]" Structurally, this schizophrenia of the grid is evident in the tension between its centrifugal and centripetal existence. While the repeated, monotonous organisation of horizontal and vertical lines suggests that the grid is merely "a tiny piece arbitrarily cropped from an infinitely larger fabric",

23 Krauss, Rosalind, *op. cit.*, p. 52.

24 *Ibid.*, p. 50.

25 Greenberg, Clement, "Modernist Painting", in Charles Harrison & Paul Wood (ed.), *Art in Theory; 1900-2000. An Anthology of Changing Ideas*, Oxford, Blackwell, 2003, p. 773-779.

26 Krauss, Rosalind, *op. cit.*, p. 52.

27 *Ibid.*, p. 54.

Fig. 3
Agnes Martin
Summer, 1964
Watercolour, ink and gouache on paper,
23.4 × 23.4 cm
Patricia Lewy Gidwitz Collection
© Sabam Belgium 2023

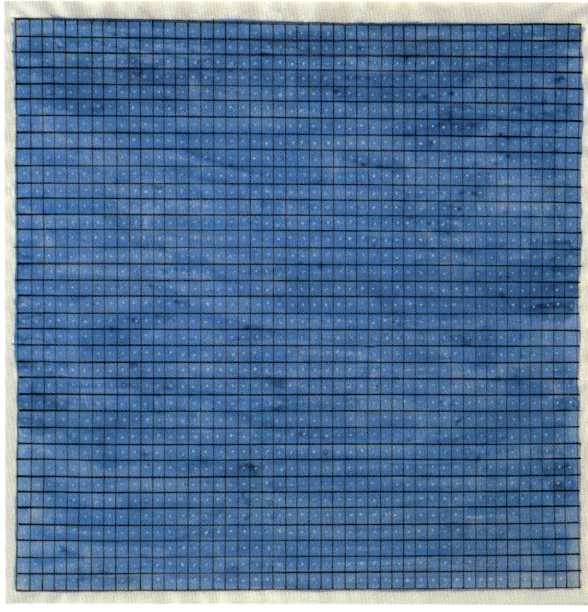

its projection onto the limited, autonomous space of the canvas, whose texture it imitates, effectively keeps it within the frame[28]. This differentiation between centrifugal and centripetal forces can be traced to an earlier debate about the grid's opposing functions between form and content, structure and narrative, and spatial and temporal phenomena. John Elderfield makes a distinction between grids as structures and grids as *frameworks*[29]. Whilst structure-grids are centripetal insofar as they constitute *"allover small-scale textures"*, insisting on their spatial, material and formal characteristics (for example, Jackson Pollock's *action painting* or the grid systems of Minimalism), framework-grids are receptacles based on the principle of an accumulation of modules holding information and potentially forming an infinite continuum (Andy Warhol's silkscreen prints or the photographic grids of Conceptual art)[30].

In her essay *Patterns, Grids, and Painting* (1975), art critic Amy Goldin reiterates this same distinction, while insisting on the centrifugal character of the grid as an anti-hierarchical, non-relational structure. By emphasising the interval at the expense of the motif, "Pattern trivializes and degrades its themes by turning them into aesthetic details within a larger, more inclusive

28 *Ibid.*, p. 60.

29 Elderfield, John, *op. cit.*, p. 53.

30 *Ibid.*, p. 54.

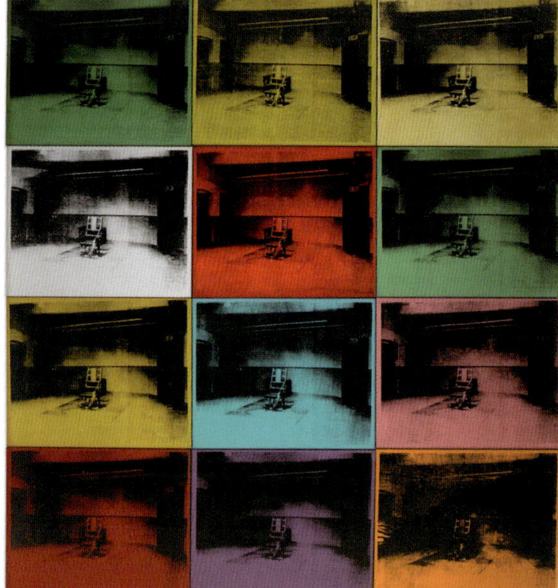

form"[31]. In this sense, Warhol's *Disaster* and *Electric Chair* series [Fig. 4] illustrate the paradox that a shocking subject loses all emotional charge when it is repeated inside an ordered, rational system. By questioning the sentiments that the grid can elicit, Goldin raises another aspect that Elderfield and Krauss do not consider, i.e., that of the viewer's emotional reaction to it. This is not insignificant since, as the critic explains, "Grids generate a greater emotional distance – a sense of the presence of objective, pervasive law." A little later, Goldin wonders how this neutral structure generates a sense of anxiety and answers the question herself by suggesting that the lack of reference marks in a regular grid engenders disorientation[32]. I believe that Goldin touches on a fundamental paradox that is perhaps at the source of the other aforementioned paradoxes, and which has been at work in every grid-based work since Cubism. The paradox between cold distance and spontaneous affect, between objective rationality and emotional sensitivity. While this debate reveals the complexity of the grid as a form and structure, it is locked in binary terms, whereby modernist art would have prioritised the rational, objective, autonomous and spatial nature of the grid, while emotion, subjectivity, narrative and temporality would have been excluded or – in Krauss's words – would

31 GOLDIN, Amy, *op. cit.*, p. 51.

32 *Ibid.*, p. 52.

Theo van Doesburg
Composition en dissonances, 1919
Oil on canvas, 64.9 × 59.6 cm
Kunstmuseum, Basel

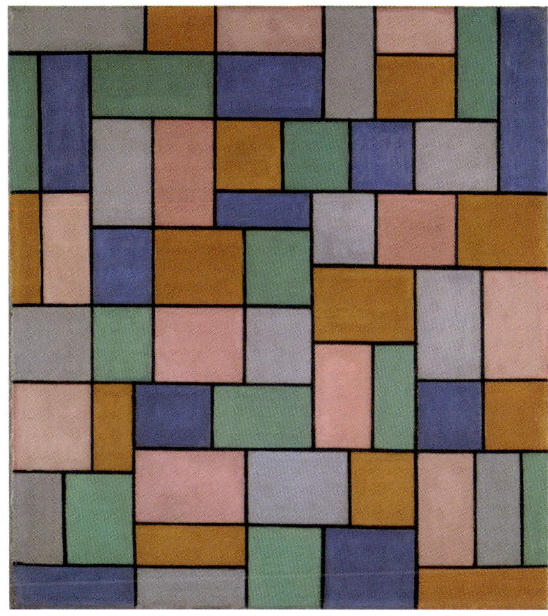

have retreated into "its unconscious, as something repressed[33]". However, it transpires that, between 1950 and 1970, many artists focused on these "repressed" qualities, by emphasising the qualities of the grid as a matrix for communication and by integrating randomness (and by extension the incalculable element) to reintroduce affect and temporality.[34]

Concrete Permutations

33 KRAUSS, Rosalind, *op. cit.*, p. 55.

34 In fact, the graphic and spatial grids created by Rodchenko and Popova in the 1920s to support the socialist revolution with their typographic, plastic and theatrical works were already designed to convey political messages and engage with the public. See Margarita Tupitsyn, "The Grid as a Checkpoint of Modernity", Tate Papers, No. 12, Autumn 2009. https://www.tate.org.uk/research/tate-papers/12/the-grid-as-a-checkpoint-of-modernity, consulted on 18 March 2023.

35 VAN DOESBURG, Theo, "Base de la peinture concrete", *Art concret*, First year, introductory issue, 1930, p. 1.

Born of the constructivist tendencies of the first half of the twentieth century, Concrete Art draws on rational, mathematical thinking and aims, in the words of Theo van Doesburg, "to be made entirely of purely plastic elements, i.e., planes and colours[35]". In his compositions from around 1920 [Fig. 5], this conception of painting as an autonomous, self-referential discipline that "has no meaning other than 'itself'" is expressed in the form of relatively uniform-coloured grids that occupy the entire surface of the canvas. The aspiration for a universal language, the primacy of intellectual control over the unpredictability of emotion, a focus on optics and mathematical construction over sensuality and fantasy… such were the precepts van Doesburg advanced about his concrete paintings, establishing them as typical examples of the Modernist paradigm[36]. Max Bill, a former Bauhaus student and, since 1932, a member of the Abstraction-création group founded by van Doesburg, used the term "concrete art" in a document published in 1936 that was subsequently revised thirteen years later. In this text, the Swiss artist emphasised the autonomy and specificity of Concrete Art as an expression of the human mind. However, the spiritual and theosophical ambitions of the De Stijl artists were being replaced by a mathematical and technological orientation. Concrete Art borrows some principles from mathematics, including geometric order, systematic seriality and modular and numerical sequences, while simultaneously establishing new aesthetic realities positioned somewhere between the intellectual, the universal, the a-natural and the unique, the individual and closeness to nature[37]. As Eduard Hüttinger explained, increasingly intricate rules can only be managed using a modular grid that enables rotations, oblique mutations, and a variety of progressions to be incorporated[38].

The serial nature of the grid and its incremental and combinatorial qualities introduce movement, individual choice, and playful pleasure, such that the result is beyond total control. While Amy Goldin has argued – alluding to Émile Zola's famous words – that "Few things on earth are more pointless than a grid seen through a temperament[39]", Bill suggests that the method of variation, whereby a basic theme is repeated in an infinite number of the most diverse developments, is conducive to individualism and temperament. The sheer play of shapes and colours that spreads through various manifestations is ultimately grounded in the bias of the personal element in composition intended to generate pleasure and individual interpretation [Fig. 6][40]. "Art plainly calls for both feeling and reasoning," says Bill in a 1949 article on the mathematical approach to contemporary art[41]. The intrusion of randomness, irrationality, and playfulness into the repetitive geometric order of the grid is evident – for example – in the painting *Le carré blanc* (1946), where the intrusion of a single white square into an arrangement of 9 x 9 black squares breaks up the monotony of the pictorial system and energises the composition, while prompting the viewer to question the meaning of this anomaly. The artist's prints and silkscreens, most often made in series, systematically and rationally explore a theme, investigating the shifting rhythms and relationships of abstract forms and taking the viewer on an exploratory journey[42]. In his seminal work *Aesthetica*, written between

36 *Ibid.*, p. 2.

37 BILL, Max, "art concret", in Eduard Hüttinger (dir.), *Max Bill*, Zurich, abc edition, 1978, p. 61.

38 HÜTTINGER, Eduard, "on the work of max bill", in Eduard Hüttinger (dir.), *op. cit.*, p. 17.

39 GOLDIN, Amy, *op. cit.*, p. 53. In 1865, Zola gives the following definition: "An artwork is a corner of creation seen through a temperament."

40 BILL, Max, "fifteen variations on a single theme (1938)", in Eduard Hüttinger (dir.), *op. cit.*, p. 68-69.

41 BILL, Max, "The mathematical approach in contemporary art (1949)", in Eduard Hüttinger (dir.), *op. cit.*, p. 110.

42 BILL, Max, "fifteen variations on a single theme (1938)", *op. cit.*, p. 112 and BILL, Jakob, "max bill und die druckgrafik", in Thomas Buchsteiner, Otto Letze (dir.), *max bill, maler, bildhauer, architekt, designer*, Ostfildern-Ruit, Hatje Cantz, 2005, p. 222.

Fig. 6

Max Bill
Untitled, 1968

Silkscreen on card, 65 × 50 cm
Inv. 2021.347
Donation Guillaume Wunsch – Monique Van Kerckhove:
Système – Hasard – Programme
© Sabam Belgium 2023. Photo Musée L / J.-P. Bougnet

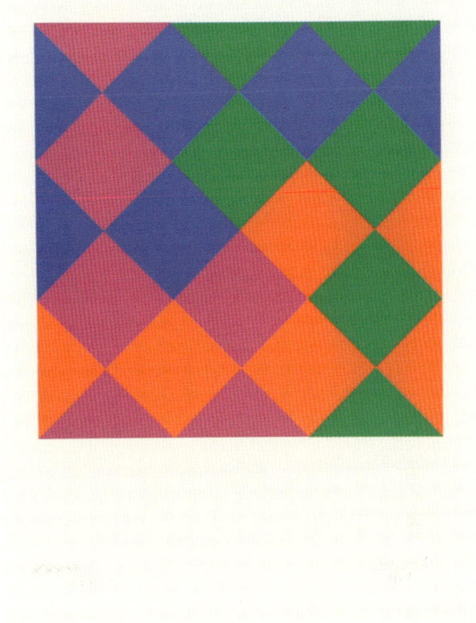

1954 and 1960, philosopher Max Bense made repeated reference to Bill's work when expanding on his idea of art as a form of information. Art, which is based on signals, signs, functions, models, grids and structures, is increasingly becoming part of modern modes of aesthetic and technical communication[43]. The grid is an informational and playful transmission system and a means of aesthetic analysis that allows us to subdivide the composition into discrete units to determine the distribution of pictorial elements[44].

This understanding of the grid as an informational matrix, which expresses abstract ideas not via objects and forms but rather through functional relationships, can be clearly traced in the graphic design of the Zurich School. Building on practices introduced at the Bauhaus and pursued by Max Bill and Richard Paul Lohse in the 1940s, Swiss graphic designers Karl Gerstner, Rosmarie Tissi, Siegfried Odermatt and Josef Müller-Brockmann developed a grid system – the typographic grid or composition grid – to control, separate, link and hierarchise the different pictorial and typographic elements on a page. Launched in 1958 by Lohse, Müller-Brockmann, Hans Neuburg and Carlo Vivarelli, the *Neue Grafik* magazine very quickly became a

43 BENSE, Max, *Aesthetica. Einführung in die neue Ästhetik*, Baden-Baden, Agis 1965. Published in 1965, the book comprises the four sections of Aesthetica, written between 1954 and 1960, and the manifesto of generative drawing.

44 *Ibid.*, p. 329-330.

major platform for modern design *made in Switzerland*, with the grid as its rational framework[45]. By dividing the page into equally proportioned zones, the grid serves to control space and make reading easier, so that the reader can immediately grasp the content. In 1961, Müller-Brockmann published his book *The Graphic Artist and His Design Problems* (1961), describing – for the first time – the grid as a fundamental principle of modern typography. By imposing a rigorous and uniform system of order on the page, Müller-Brockmann argued that the grid represents a constructive attitude and facilitates the objective organisation of arguments, a logical presentation of texts and images, and the clear and transparent communication of visual information. In this, concludes the graphic designer, the grid "constitutes the basis of democratic behaviour"[46]. In the aftermath of the Second World War and the height of the Cold War, the grid was regarded as a simultaneously aesthetic and political medium that provided a perfect balance between collective uniformity and individual freedom[47]. In modern design, the compositional grid is not envisaged as a neutral, self-referential framework, but as a social and political form aimed at clear, intelligible communication of a scripted and visual message. Unlike Krauss's supposed anti-narrative character, the grid assumes a function that structures and supports the narrative. As Timothy Samara points out:

"A grid is truly successful only if, after all of the literal problems have been solved, the designer rises above the uniformity implied by its structure and uses it to create a dynamic visual narrative of parts that will sustain interest page after page[48]."

(De)generative Variations

In the early 1960s, Generative or Digital Art simultaneously surfaced in the United States and at the University of Stuttgart (TH Stuttgart), where Bense occupied a chair in philosophy and scientific theory from 1949. In February 1965, the first known exhibition of digital art took place in the Studiengalerie of the TH Stuttgart. Using a Siemens 2002 computer and a drawing machine – the Graphomat Z64 –one of Bense's students, Georg Nees, produced a series of graphics based on arithmetic operations that generated unprecedented geometric patterns. Using random generators, Nees introduced the unexpected and distortions into these programmed images, thereby transforming them into aesthetic artefacts. Like his mentor Bense, Nees based

45 Hollis, Richard, *Le Graphisme. De 1890 à nos jours*, London, Thames & Hudson, 2002, p. 132-133.

46 Müller-Brockmann, Josef, *Rastersysteme für die visuelle Gestaltung. Ein Handbuch für Grafiker*, Typografen und Ausstellungsgestalter, Niggli, Salenstein, 1996, p. 10.

47 Gerstner, Karl, *Designing Programmes* (1968), quoted in Timothy Samara, *Making and Breaking the Grid*, Cloucester, MA, Rockport, 2002, p. 19.

48 Samara, Timothy, *ibid.*, p. 30.

Fig. 7

Georg Nees
Schotter, 1969

Lithograph in black ink on paper, mounted on card,
28 × 21.8 cm
© Victoria and Albert Museum, London

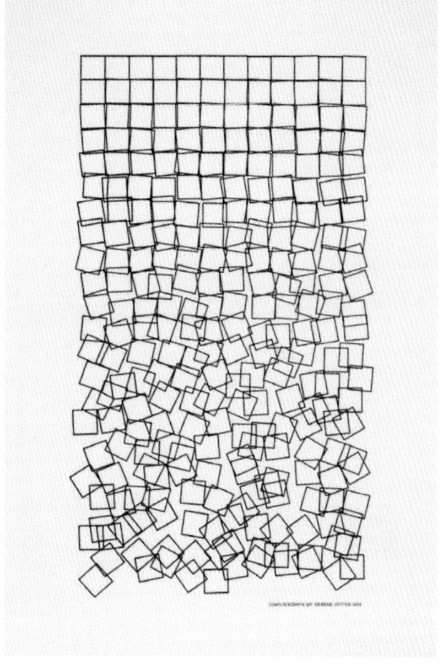

his work on the idea that the relationship between order and disorder underlying information theory is also a key aspect of aesthetic production. In *Aesthetica*, Bense uses the term "artificial art" to define this new computer-generated art. Unlike "natural art", such as painting for example, digital art brings an intermediary scheme, the programming language, between the artist and his artwork[49]. In *Schotter* (1969) [Fig. 7], this algorithmic layer automates the creative process, transforming the composition of a regular grid into a mass of chaotic squares by moving and rotating its modules.

Inspired by Bense's writings and spurred on by Pierre Barbaud, a pioneer of algorithmic music, Manfred Mohr composed his first generative drawings in 1969. In his manifesto for a programmed aesthetic, the artist states that, in digital art, the whole of forms replaces the single form, and the relational principle replaces singularity, in such a way that the totality of possible combinations represents a "quality of a quantity", placing redundancy, statistics, repetition, infinity and the structuring of information at the heart of artistic investigation[50]. It is therefore hardly surprising that the grid should become a generative matrix onto which the artist propagates "graphic beings" using

49 BENSE, Max, *op. cit.*, p. 338.
See also: VON HERRMANN, Hans-Christian, "Künstliche Kunst – eine strukturalistische Tätigkeit", in Hans-Christian von Herrmann and Christoph Hoffmann (ed.), *Georg Nees. Generative Computergraphik*, Berlin, Vice Versa, 2006, p. 30.

50 MOHR, Manfred, "Artist's Statement", in Pierre Gaudibert (ed.), *Manfred Mohr Computer Graphics – Une esthétique programmée*, cat., ARC, Musée d'Art moderne de la Ville de Paris, 1971, p. 36-40.

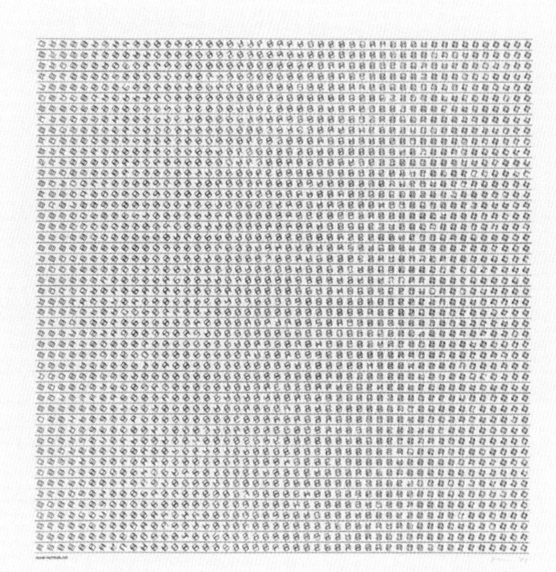

systematic and random procedures. The *CUBIC LIMIT I* series [Fig. 8], made between 1973 and 1975, is founded on the innumerable combinations of the twelve lines of a three-dimensional cube understood as numerical values. The integration of these syntactic elements into an orthogonal grid emphasises the redundant, repetitive, and infinite nature of these "graphic beings", while simultaneously transforming them into "iconic signs" that refer back to their existence as meaningful aesthetic forms[51]. But the grid is not just a rational, inflexible mould that compartmentalises and fixes the forms generated on the computer, but it is also a matrix for interpretation that is both decisive and open: "On a global level, within the given field-structure (matrix) of my drawings the basic neighbourhood relationships of the signes [SIC] generate either cluster or linear 'readings'[52]." With its multiple reading possibilities (vertical, horizontal, diagonal, etc.), the grid constitutes the perfect model for conceiving the artwork in terms of aesthetic communication.

In his book *The Open Work*, first published in 1962, Umberto Eco differentiates between the "meaning" and the "information" contained in a message. While meaning "is a function of the order, the conventions, and the redundancy of its structure"

51 Mohr, Manfred *Cubic Limit*, cat., galerie Pierre Weiller, 29 May – 28 June 1975, Paris, n.p.

52 *Ibid.*

Fig. 9

François Morellet
2 doubles trames -1° +1° moirées, c. 1971

Silkscreen on paper, 49.5 × 49.5 cm
Inv. 2021.323
Donation Guillaume Wunsch – Monique Van Kerckhove:
Système – Hasard – Programme
© Sabam Belgium 2023. Photo Musée L / J.-P. Bougnet

based on "preestablished principles that guide the organization of a message and are reiterated via the repetition of foreseeable elements", information is "understood as potential, as the inception of possible orders" drawing on the improbability, the ambiguity and the disordered structure of the message.[53] Born of the tension between these two poles – order and disorder – each artwork can be viewed as a message that "appears ambiguous and open-ended".[54] On the occasion of the exhibition *Arte Programmata*, held at the Galleria Vittorio Emanuele in Milan from 12 to 26 May 1962, Umberto Eco applied his concept of the aesthetic message to programmed art, which he described as a "singular dialectic between case and programme, between mathematics and chance, between planned conception and free acceptance of what happens [...]"[55].

These ideas about the programmed work as an open work can also be found in the projects of GRAV (Groupe de recherche d'Art visuel), an artists' collective founded in Paris in 1960. François Morellet, one of the group's founders, emphasised the constructed and programmed nature of the work, which, through the integration of random operations and optical effects [Fig. 9] (moirés, shimmers, diffraction, interference, etc.), introduced movement

53 ECO, Umberto, *The Open Work*, Harvard University Press, Cambridge, Massachusetts, 1989, p. 93.

54 *Ibid.*, p. 195.

55 Eco quoted in HOHLFELDT, Marion and IMBERNON, Laurence (ed.), *Mouvement, lumière, participation. GRAV 1960-1968*, cat., Rennes, Édition galerie Art & Essai, 2013, p. 104.

and instability, thereby inviting the public to take an active part: "A true experiment must [...] be conducted on the basis of controllable elements, progressing systematically according to a programme. [...] This programmed experimental painting seems to meet [the] public's need [...] to take part in the 'creation' of the artworks[56]". Vera Molnár, another of the group's founders, made her first digital works in 1968 when she was given access to a computer at the Bull Information Systems research centre in Paris. She saw the computer as a liberating tool whose "immense combinatory capacity facilitates the systematic investigation of the infinite field of possibilities[57]".

Applying the trial-and-error method, the artist uses random generators to obtain countless unpredicted variations of a motif, selecting a few to create her paintings based on her own subjective taste. The simulation of intuition by random algorithms dictates the intuitive and subjective choice of the artist, who in turn provides the instructions for the computer programme on which the work is based. Drawing inspiration from cybernetics and information theory, Molnár describes this process as "visual feedback", i.e., a creative feedback effect under which the artist's imagination is fed by the computer's arithmetic operations, and vice versa[58]. Molnár's mid-1970s acrylic paintings entitled *Computer Icône* based on a series of computer printouts are the outcome of this visual feedback process. The 1977 painting *100 carrés jaunes (computer icône 3)* [cat., p. 68] is composed of a Senegal Yellow background on which an irregular orthogonal grid of 10 x 10 squares, painted in a different hue of the same colour, is drawn. The level of disorder and distribution of the individual tones are determined partly by chance, transforming the grid into a pulsating surface, into a veritable icon of generative painting at the intersection between static form and dynamic process, between mathematical system and artistic intuition, and between algorithmic calculation and subjective imagination.

Concept, Series, System

In the 1960s, the theories of cybernetics, communication, and information were also in vogue in American Conceptual Art. The exhibitions *Software, Information Technology: Its New Meaning of Art* and *Information*, both held in 1970, outlined the new "sense of communication" in the art of the time[59]. By focusing on the relationship between art and technology, Jack Burnham, who curated *Software*, uses the notion of "software" as a metaphor

56 MORELLET, François, *Groupe de recherche d'art visuel* (plaquette), Paris, galerie Denise René and the GRAV, 1962, n. p.

57 MOLNÁR, Vera, "Regards sur mes images" (1984). http://www.veramolnar.com/blog/wp-content/uploads/VM1984_regards.pdf, consulted on 18 March 2023.

58 On the influence of cybernetics and information theory on Molnár, see GUILLEMET, Aline, "Vera Molnár Computer Paintings", *Representations*, February 2020, 1-30.

59 MCSHINE, Kynaston (ed.), *Information*, cat., Museum of Modern Art, New York, 1970, p. 141.

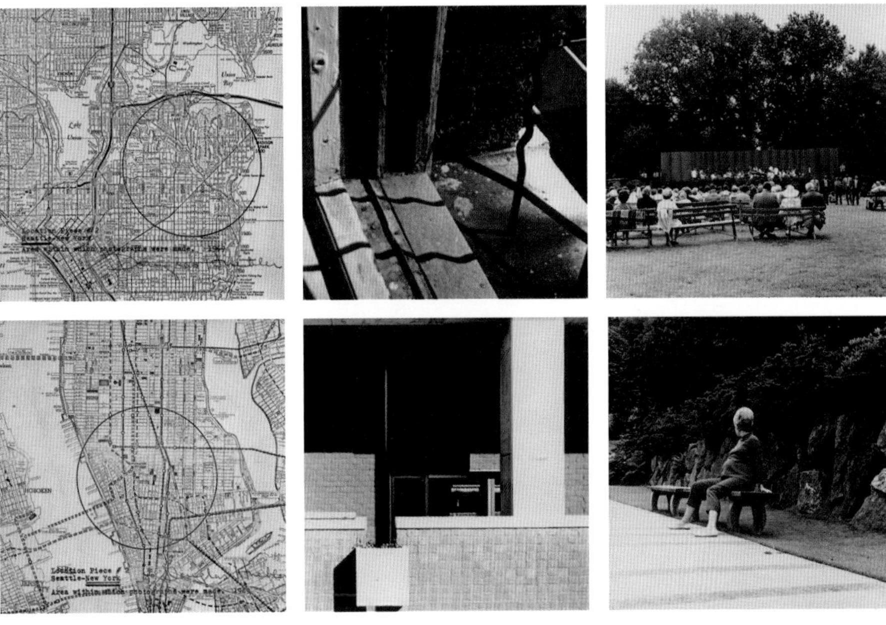

Fig. 10

Douglas Huebler
Location Piece #2,
New York, Seattle, Washington, 1970
Offset print on card, 18 × (18 × 18 cm)
Inv. 2022.36
Artists and Photographs, New York, Marian Goodman,
1970
© Sabam Belgium 2023. Photo Musée L

60 SHAKEN, Edward A., "Art in the
Information Age: Technology and
Conceptual Art", *Leonardo*, Vol. 35,
No. 4, 2002, p. 434.

61 BOCHNER, Mel, "The Serial Attitude",
Artforum, December 1967, p. 28.

62 *Ibid.*, p. 27.

for the way in which artists approach "information systems and their devices"[60]. In this context, the grid constitutes an omnipresent matrix to represent "information systems", shifting from the checkerboard arrangement of images to the highlighting of the reproduction grid or the computer grid, from the cartographic grid to the urban and architectural grid. In his paper *The Serial Attitude*, Mel Bochner argued that serial art is abstract, autonomous and non-referential. Serial order, seen as a method rather than a style, is thought to be based on three operating assumptions: a numerical or systematically predetermined process (permutation, progression, rotation, inversion), the primacy of order over execution, and systematic self-exhaustion[61]. These criteria are the same as those invoked by the protagonists of Concrete Art and Generative Art. But for Bochner, the referent of the serial system is not found in the abstract realm of mathematical calculation, but in the external world, made intelligible by the serial order of the grid. In cartography, for instance, "Parallels of latitude, isobars, isothermal lines and other grid coordinate denotations, all serialized, are further cases of the application of external structure systems to order the unordered.[62]" Douglas Huebler, On Kawara, John Baldessari and many other conceptual artists incorporated the geographical map or the city plan

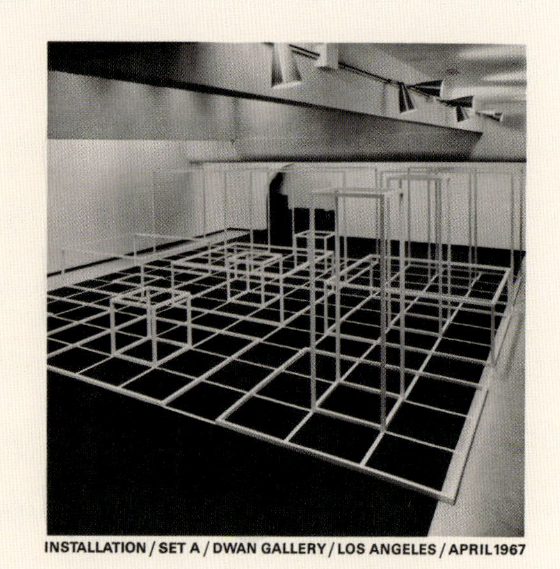

Fig. 11

Sol LeWitt
Serial Project #1, Set A, 1967
Los Angeles, Dwan Gallery
Museo Reina Sofía. Collección Archivo Lafuente
© Sabam Belgium 2023

into their series of works as a means of exploring the differences between the appropriation of a terrain by the cartographic grid as an abstract and symbolic system of information, and the exploration of that same terrain through bodily and subjective experience. Moreover, these maps or plans are frequently displayed along with photographs, organised in series or in a grid, combining two systems of representation and appropriation of space: the photograph as an indexical trace, capable of documenting reality, and the map as a graphic projection of the world reproducing topographical and geographical details, while also reflecting political, economic and social realities [Fig. 10].

One of the artworks included in Bochner's article as an example of "serial logics" is *Serial Project #1, Set A* [Fig. 11], exhibited by Sol LeWitt at the Dwan Gallery in Los Angeles in 1967. This piece is composed of a network of squares, which occupy a large part of the gallery floor, and on which a complex system of open forms is deployed according to a rational, progressive logic. LeWitt's handwritten instructions, appended to the diagram on the invitation card, specify that "the cube, square and variants on them are used as grammatical devices" and that the underlying "grid system is a convenience. It stabilizes the measurements and neutralizes space by treating it equally[63]." Such use of the square and the cube as basic elements that have no value except inside a modular system is, of course, at odds with the traditional aesthetic categories of taste, originality, and the autonomy of art. LeWitt tells us that the

63 LEGG, Alicia (ed.), *Sol LeWitt,* cat., The Museum of Modern Art, New York, 1978, p. 72.

serial artist is merely a "clerk cataloguing the results of his premise[64]." While Dan Graham describes the *STRUCTURAL GRID* as a pre-established matrix that sets up an interplay of "discontinuous oppositions", he compares it to structuralist theories, according to which meaning does not reside in the phenomena themselves, but in the relationships between them within a system of differences[65]. So it is not so much the cube (or square) that forms the substance of LeWitt's work, but rather the interval that organises and determines the position of the elementary units. However, Graham exposes an interesting paradox when he fully acknowledges the objectifying and self-defining nature of LeWitt's work, while simultaneously stressing its complex relationship with the interior of the gallery and the public. Situated between the second and third dimensions, the grid both represents the interior space of the gallery and the idea that begins with the line. On the one hand, the bars, as the framework of the work, literally forbid the viewer access to the interior of the grid, which is presented as an autonomous system. On the other, the potential limitlessness of the work understood in terms of a repetition of intervals prolongs the piece in space, piercing the viewer like a transparent projection[66].

These considerations on the relationship between work, surrounding space, and spectator suggest that it would be wrong to reduce LeWitt's modular structures to autonomous conceptual systems disconnected from any external reality. In reality, their skeletal framework relates to a very specific context: namely, the architectural grid, the symbol of American rationalism dominating New York City's urban landscape, with its grid system peppered with skeletons of steel and the orthogonal façades of its skyscrapers. LeWitt's fascination with the architectural structures around him is evident in the modular structures created in the shape of a step pyramid (ziggurat). In 1966, the artist published an article on the ziggurat, a shape of office building that was extremely fashionable in New York between 1916 and 1963, on account of the city planning code that stipulated that buildings above a certain height had to be set back to allow for light and air circulation. LeWitt espoused this type of administrative constraint, arguing that the somewhat rigid code would prevent an aestheticism excessively dependent on individual taste, while simultaneously providing enough flexibility to accommodate considerable creative freedom[67]. The idea of constraint as a liberating principle also applies to the grid as a modular matrix from which different variations can be derived.

While the link between the grid and the urban environment remains implicit in the 1960s sculptures, it becomes abundantly

64 LeWitt, Sol, "Serial Project No. 1 (ABCD)", in Alicia Legg (ed.), *op. cit.*, p. 170.

65 Graham, Dan, "Information" (1967/1969), in Dan Graham, *For Publication*, Gallery, Otis Art Institute of Los Angeles County, 1975, n. p. On the influence of structuralism on conceptual art, see Eve Meltzer, *Systems We Have Loved: Conceptual Art, Affect, and the Antihumanist Turn*, Chicago and London, The University of Chicago Press, 2013, p. 17-18.

66 Graham, Dan, "Two Structures/Sol LeWitt", in Birgit Pelzer, Mark Francis, Beatriz Colomina (ed.), *Dan Graham*, London, New York, Phaidon, 2001, p. 100.

67 LeWitt, Sol, "Ziggurats" (1966), in Alicia Legg (ed.), *op. cit.*, 172-173.

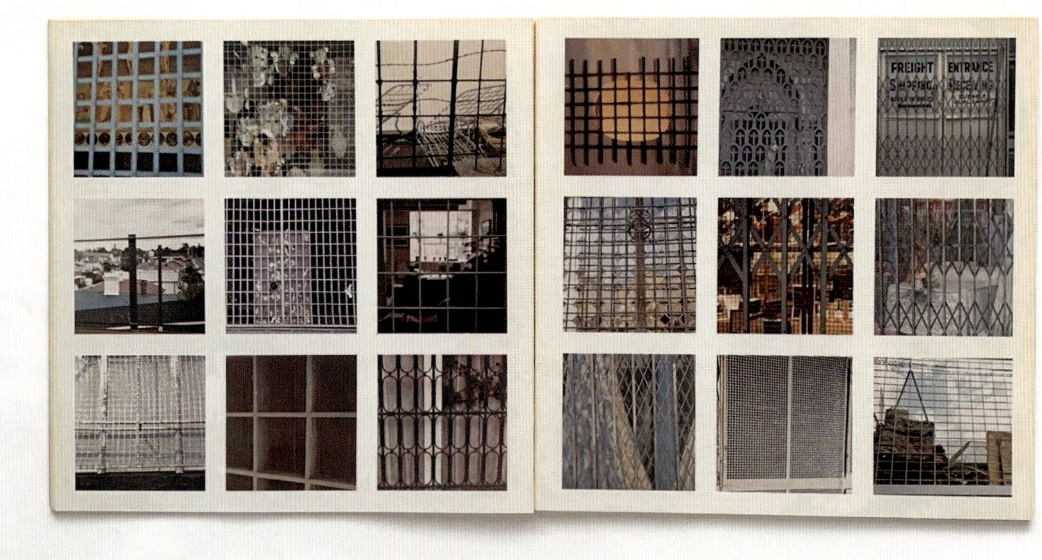

clear in the photographic books produced by the artist in the late 1970s. In particular, *Photogrids* (1977) [Fig. 12] contains 414 square photographs, with each page featuring a grid of nine images. Arranged thematically, the images depict various types of grids found by the artist in urban spaces while travelling to install his *wall drawings*. LeWitt laconically described his approach: "No matter where one looks in an urban city there are grids to be seen[68]". And indeed, the book features a vast assortment of grids: coffered doors, window grilles, trellises, manhole covers, cobbled streets, brick walls, squared-off facades, steel bridges, even street games such as hopscotch, a lumberjack shirt, and a calculator. The fact that this eclectic accumulation of objects and grid-like motifs also encompasses several sculptures made by LeWitt and his friend Carl Andre confirms that LeWitt does not consider his works as purely mental objects, neutral and autonomous, removed from any historical, economic, or socio-cultural context. Renaissance cathedrals, children's games, human constructions, and clothes, all kinds of protective and enclosing devices, or even tools for ciphering the world, all reveal that the grid is very much an apparatus in the sense given to the term by Giorgio Agamben, i.e., something that has "the capacity to capture, orient, determine, intercept,

Fig. 12

Sol LeWitt
Photogrids, 1977
Artist's book, published by Paul Davis Press / Rizzoli, New York, 26 × 26.5 cm
Inv. 2021.481
Donation Guillaume Wunsch – Monique Van Kerckhove: Système – Hasard – Programme
© Sabam Belgium 2023. Photo Musée L

68 LEGG, Alicia (ed.), *op. cit.*, p. 158.

model, control, or secure the gestures, behaviors, opinions, or discourses of living beings.[69]"

The Photographic Grid as Exhibition

LeWitt's book is presented as a double grid: on the one hand, the motifs represented and, on the other, the way the photographs are organised on the page. In other terms, as a medium of reproduction and multiplication, photography gives us an indispensable reading grid for collecting, organising, categorising, classifying and interpreting all the grids we come across in the world, which organise and order our daily lives, and quite literally give them structure. In the 1960s, photography became the preferred medium for Conceptual Art, due to its ability to document, reproduce, and multiply the world. For many artists, such as Bernd and Hilla Becher, Douglas Huebler, Andy Warhol, Robert Smithson, Eleanor Antin, Martha Wilson, Christian Boltanski, Peter Feldmann and others, the photographic grid emerged as the ideal device for the spatio-temporal, serial or typological organisation of reality. This is all the more remarkable given that photography has rarely been subject to studies on the grid[70]. Symptomatically, the only specific reference to photography in the discussions of the 1970s described above comes in a footnote. This footnote, in John Elderfield's text, is nonetheless worth noting. Elderfield likens photography to the grid as a means of transfer and quotes American philosopher Stanley Cavell: the "implied presence of the rest of the world, and its explicit rejection, are as essential in the experience of a photograph as what it explicitly presents...[71]"

Like the grid, photography is centripetal insofar as it is determined by its frame, and centrifugal, since, to quote Susan Sontag, "one photograph, unlike one painting, implies that there will be others.[72]" Moreover, as a means of reproduction and multiplication, photography converts "the world into a department store or museum-without-walls in which every subject is depreciated into an article of consumption, promoted into an item for aesthetic appreciation[73]". Evidently, this *"museum-without-walls"* refers to André Malraux's imaginary museum. Based on the observation that the history of modern art "is the history of *what can be photographed*", Malraux envisaged the photographic album as a closed world that brought together on the same scale artworks of extremely different types, functions and sizes, originating from separate geographical areas, to form a comparative universe where "the model becomes the means of the image far more

69 Agamben, Giorgio, *What is an Apparatus? and Other Essays*, Stanford, California, Stanford University Press, 2009, p. 14.

70 Claus Gunti acknowledges this shortcoming when he notes that Krauss and others would have considered non-photographic art exclusively. Gunti, Claus, *Digital Image Systems. Photography and New Technologies at the Düsseldorf School*, Bielefeld, transcript, 2019, p. 134.

71 Cavell, Stanley, *The World Viewed. Reflections on the Ontology of Film*, New York, Cambridge, MA, Harvard University Press, 1979, p. 24. Elderfield, *op. cit.*, p. 59.

72 Sontag, Susan, *On Photography*, New York, Dell Publishing Company, 1977, p. 166.

73 *Ibid.*, p. 126-127.

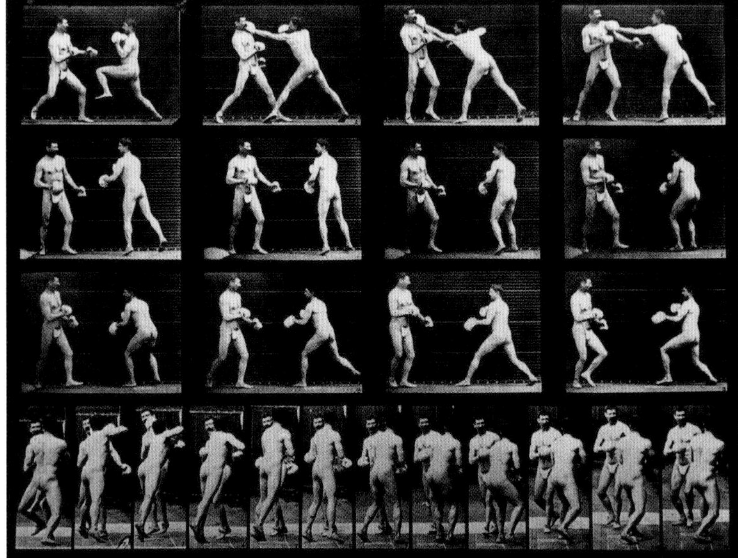

Fig. 13

Eadweard Muybridge
Boxing with Gloves, from the *Animal Locomotion* series,
volume V. *Plate 335*, 1887

Silver gelatin print, modern print,
23.7 × 31.7 cm
Musée de la Photographie de Charleroi Collection

than the image is the reproduction of the model.[74]" Maurice Jarnoux's iconic photograph of Malraux in his living room, surrounded by a multitude of photographic reproductions laid out on the floor following a rectangular pattern, clearly shows that the preferred mode of presentation in his imaginary museum is the grid. From this angle, LeWitt's *Photogrids* represents an imaginary museum that, through the square arrangement of its various grids, reveals its own function as an exhibition device.

Thus, the photography grid introduces a system of comparison enabling the objects reproduced to be examined across space and time. In order to systematically explore this spatio-temporal dimension of photography, Sol LeWitt, Dan Graham, and other artists drew inspiration from Eadweard Muybridge's chronophotography. In the late 1870s, Muybridge devised a battery of several cameras triggered in succession, to decompose the movements of an animal or a person scientifically. In his book *Animal Locomotion* [Fig. 13], published in 1887, the photographs are arranged in 781 plates, each of which displays shots of the same subject, captured at different moments, in an orthogonal grid. In his writings, conceptual artist Dan Graham makes several references to Muybrigde's work, which he finds inspiring in terms of its

74 Malraux, André, *Le musée imaginaire*, Paris, Gallimard, 1965, p. 84 and p. 111.

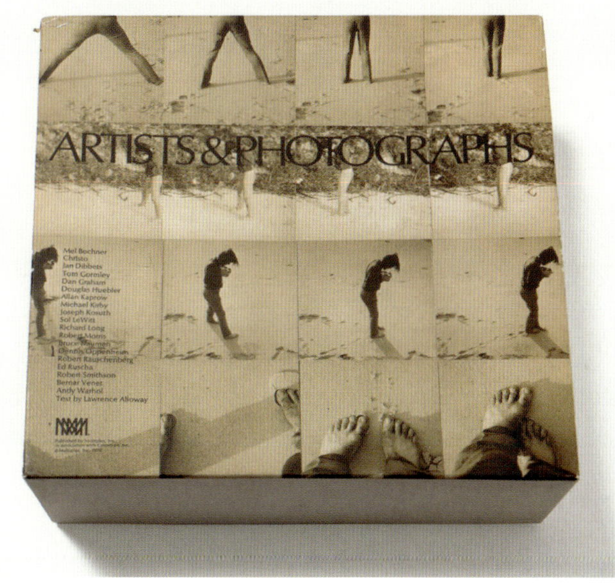

Fig. 14

Dan Graham
Artists and Photographs, 1970
Miniature exhibition in a box, 19 contributing artists,
text by Lawrence Alloway, cardboard box,
cover designed by Dan Graham, 33.7 × 33.7 × 9.5 cm
Printed by Colorcraft, Inc. in New York; published by
Multiples in association with Colorcraft Inc, New York
Courtesy The Estate of Dan Graham and Multiples, Inc.
© The Estate of Dan Graham and Multiples, Inc. /
Marian Goodman Gallery. Photo Cathy Carver

scientific, serial, and multi-perspective aspects. Muybridge used a mesh screen in front of which he paraded his models, Graham observes, to obtain exact calculations of the relationship between the moving body, time, and the perspective system[75]. By contrast, the arrangement of images in superimposed sequences removes the fixed point of view of central perspective and breaks down space "into a number of overlapping reference points – mapped 'points of interest' – in a two-dimensional point to point 'grid'".[76] The collapse of Renaissance spatial illusionism goes hand in hand with a multiplication and a fragmentation of space-time. When Dan Graham created the cover work for the multiple *Artists and Photographs* [Fig. 14], edited by Marian Goodman and published in 1970, he must have had this in mind. Consisting of a checkerboard of four times four images, the piece places the artist's body in a system of temporal and spatial coordinates without a fixed point of view. While three sequences depict Graham pointing his camera towards the ground from different angles, a fourth sequence reveals the images that the artist himself has taken of his feet. Unlike Muybridge's chronophotography, this multiplication of viewpoints does not only concern the positions of the body being photographed, but also the position of the subject taking the photographs. The photographic device allows Graham to abandon

75 GRAHAM, Dan, "Photographs of Motion" (1967/69), in Birgit Pelzer, Mark Francis, Beatriz Colomina (ed.), *op. cit.*, p. 106.

76 GRAHAM, Dan, "Two Parallel Essays: Two Related Projects for Slide Projector & Photographs of Motion", in *Artists and Photographs*, Marian Goodman Gallery, New York, 1970, p. 3.

the fixed point of view inside the image for a multifocal perspective, which includes the movement of the viewer's eyes as they take in the piece over time[77]. By emulating a documentary and scientific approach, shattering the central perspective and moving from the spatial and immobile painting to the temporal and cinematographic sequence, the chronophotographic grid helps Conceptual Art to escape the shackles of traditional aesthetics.

The Metrological Grid Under the Scrutiny of Feminist Critique

As Tom Gunning rightly observed, Muybridge's orthonormal grid enables the human body to navigate in the space-time of modernity, ushered in by technological progress, scientific rationality, and the mathematical calculations of modern life[78]. However, this system of reference points dates back to John Lamprey's ethnographic and anthropological practice, which was introduced in 1869 with the aim of obtaining reliable anatomical and physiological measurements for the study, classification, and comparison of living species[79]. As part of the ideology of evolutionary anthropology, this metrological grid system was intended to provide a rational and pseudo-objective framework to demonstrate the superiority of the white man and serve as a justification for colonialism. Photographs were often arranged in a grid in the physical anthropology albums. Stripped of their names and individual identities, the subjects portrayed were reduced to specimens to be collected, categorised and controlled by the Western eye. Photography became "a theatre for the staging and reinforcement of colonial asymmetry[80]". Under the guise of science, the photographic grid also played a considerable role in the nascent field of criminology, not least in the research of Italian physician Cesare Lombroso. The *Atlas* that accompanied his book *Criminal Man* published in 1876 to defend the thesis that delinquency depends on physiological and anatomical characteristics contains several plates showing different kinds of criminals: German, Russian and Italian criminals, the criminally insane, wild criminals, murderous criminals, revolutionaries and political criminals (classified as criminals of passion and moral lunatics).

This historical context provides a backdrop for some feminist initiatives that use photographic grids to challenge either the methods of positivist science or the idea of the autonomous work of art, both of which are dismissed as repressive forms of a

77 GRAHAM, Dan, "Photographs of Motion" (1967/69), *op. cit.*, p. 106.

78 GUNNING, Tom, "Never Seen This Picture Before", in David Campany (ed.), *The Cinematic*, Cambridge, MA, MIT Press, 2007, p. 21.

79 BRAUN, Marta, "Muybridge le magnifique", *Études photographiques*, n° 10 November 2001, p. 13.

80 PINNEY, Christopher, *Photography and Anthropology*, London, Reaction books, 2011, p. 48.

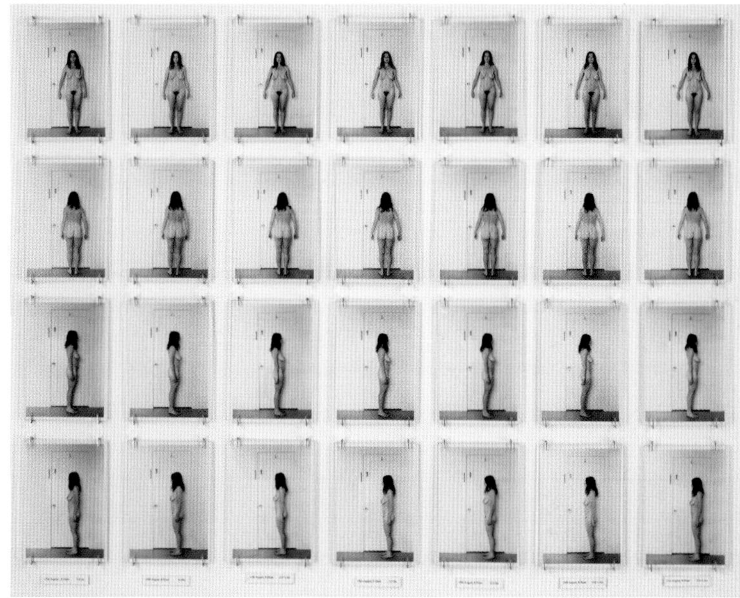

81 Foucault, Michel, "Subject and
Power", in Paul Rabinow and Hubert
L. Dreyfus (ed.), *The Foucault Reader.
An Introduction to Foucault's Thought*,
London, Penguin, p. 174. Also see:
Streitberger, Alexander, "Staged
Bodies. La double mise en scène
corporelle et photographique dans
l'art postmoderniste", in Alexander
Streitberger and Clémentine Roche (ed.),
*Staged Bodies. Mise en scène du corps
dans la photographie postmoderniste*,
Ghent, Snoeck, 2020, p. 18.

patriarchal society. In 1973, Eleanor Antin produced *Carving: A Traditional Sculpture* [Fig. 15], a piece that comprises 144 photographs, arranged in four rows of 38 images each, documenting the drastic diet she followed between 15 July and 21 August 1972. However, it is not simply a documentation of her (ironic) attempt to adapt her body to the ideal of Greek sculpture. Instead, by systematically showing the artist's naked body from the front, the back and both profiles, the series mimics the aesthetics, techniques, and devices of legal and ethnographic photography, as they were established in the nineteenth century to measure, categorise, and control the bodies of deviants and outcasts. Analogously, the female body is also subjected to a dominant ideological discourse that, to quote Foucault, deploys a whole "range of specific mechanisms and technologies" designed to enshrine its norms and rules in the bodies and behaviour of each individual[81]. This condemnation of the female body's subordination to a statistical and normative logic can also be found in Esther Ferrer's photographs of one of her first performances, *Íntimo y personal (Intimate and Personal)* (1977) [cat. p. 112]. In this series of images, the artist is depicted measuring her naked body and covering her breasts and belly with the words "intimate" and "personal". The rigid structure of the grid and the scientific method of measurement are at odds with words that assert self-determination and the right to one's own body.

Paradoxically, here the grid is exposed as an ideological tool, whilst simultaneously providing a creative departure from traditional aesthetics. With its anti-hierarchical nature and (potentially) infinite structure, the grid becomes a liberating tool for some feminist artists wanting to break away from the shackles of patriarchal society. Artists such as Gina Pane, Martha Wilson and Athiná Tácha play on the multidirectional nature of the grid to avoid subordinating the female body to a precise order that imposes a reading from left to right and top to bottom. For example, Gina Pane's *Action Transfert* [cat., p. 106] comprises twelve photographs taken in the context of the artist's performance of *Action Transfert* on 19 April 1973 at Space 640 in Saint-Jeannet[82]. During this performance, Pane broke two glasses, one full of mint water – symbolising unfulfilled desire – and the other containing milk representing childish regression. By licking the liquids mixed with the glass shards, the artist is adding her own blood, thereby revealing the violent, destructive potential at work in a society where individual desires and feelings are repressed for the sake of maintaining a rational, scientific order. Yet the arrangement of the twelve photographs does not allow us to reconstruct the temporal sequence of the action or the spatial layout of the objects. While ten close-up shots of two filled glasses and the artist in full action convey the worrying, threatening dimension of the performance, two landscape views disrupt this documentary logic to open up a poetic, suggestive space that transcends any rational, objective framework. The corporeal excesses of the action are mirrored in the excesses of the grid, which pushes back its own limits and establishes a network of relationships where the images converse with one another without being assigned a fixed meaning or place.

Memory Grids

In the early 1970s, Christian Boltanski started producing his *Albums photographiques*, followed by his *Inventaires*. In both groups of artworks, the way in which objects and images were presented mimicked anthropological and ethnological methods, except that the showcases and photographic grids did not dehumanise individuals that, deprived of their names and contexts, were transformed into anonymous racial specimens. Quite the opposite, the *Inventaires*, which are made up of objects and

82 See PLUCHART, François, "L'espace mental de Gina Pane", *arTitudes*, No. 5, Summer 1973, p. 16-19.

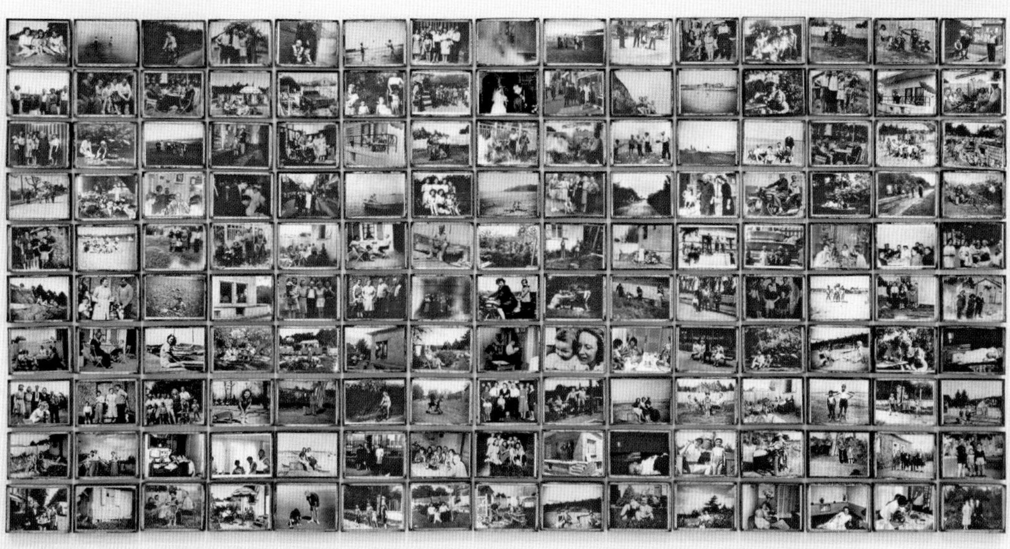

Fig. 16

Christian Boltanski
L'Album de photos de la famille D., 1939-1964, 1971
Installation, 150 black and white prints framed in tin,
220 × 450 cm
Musée d'Art moderne et contemporain de Saint-Étienne
Métropole © Sabam Belgium 2023. Photo Yves Bresson

83 BOLTANSKI, Christian and GRENIER, Catherine, *La Vie possible de Christian Boltanski*, Paris, Seuil, 2007, p. 77.

84 BOLTANSKI, Christian, *Les Modèles – cinq relations entre texte & image*, Paris, Cheval d'Attaque, 1979, p. 8. Sociologist Pierre Bourdieu argues that this identification with other people's family album photos is rooted in the fact that these images are all based on the same system of conventions, and that "the significance of the pose adopted for the photograph can only be grasped in relation to the symbolic system [in this case the family album] in which it is embedded". Pierre Bourdieu, *Un art moyen*, Paris, Seuil, 1965, p. 116.

furniture that once belonged to an anonymous person, are reminders of our own everyday lives, and thus create an emotional bond with this person reconstituted in hollow form. The interesting aspect of inventories, says Boltanski, "is that everyone looking at them sees their own portrait, because we all own more or less the same objects[83]". Whereas the physical anthropology grid establishes a distance between us, and the people represented, transforming them into subjects for study, the grid of the *Inventaires* and *Albums photographiques* has the opposite effect, because the reconstruction of the lives of anonymous people is also the reconstruction of our own lives. In *L'Album de photos de la famille D.,* 1939-1964 (1971) [Fig. 16], Boltanski took images from the family album of a close friend before reconstructing their chronological order by incorporating them into a photographic wall made up of several rows. The artist is fascinated by the contradictory feeling we experience when we look at these anonymous images, which are simultaneously alien to us, because they show a family that is completely unknown to us, and familiar, in that we recognise the poses and themes of "these images of family rituals [...] that take us back to our own memories[84]". Formally, the *Albums photographiques* underline this ambiguity by using the grid as an open and closed structure that can be read linearly or omnidirectionally. By enlarging, framing and grouping the images, the family album becomes a physical monument, a place of remembrance, which reminds us of the shared nature of our experiences, while also paying tribute to the individuals that photography has transformed into "cultural models", of whom all that remains is a faint memory.

With the advent of digital technology, the grid as memory matrix has become part of the computer's virtual space. In his piece *Memory Grid* [cat., p. 140], Michael Ensdorf investigates the consequences of digital technology in terms of facial recognition and the workings of our visual memory. The piece is made up of twenty-five anonymous portraits that have been reworked on a computer before being assembled in a grid echoing the pixel structure that underpins all digital images. Simultaneously a formal, technical and mnemonic matrix, *Memory Grid* sheds light on the grid through which objects and individuals are identified, classified and archived. The unnatural colours and pixelation resulting from the enlargement of low-resolution images demonstrate the artificial nature of these portraits that – rather than reflecting reality – only provide a quantity of information that can be manipulated and exploited. Unlike Boltanski's *Albums photographiques*, these images no longer refer to cultural rituals whereby the portrait is anchored in a specific historical, social and material context. In the words of the artist, the question posed by these immaterial portraits is "what visual information is required for a person to make a positive ID, to tricker a memory, to spark a connection?[85]" Inside the computer grid, the portrait's function is no longer simply representing a physical person, but rather forming part of a largely automated process of identification, distribution and archiving. In other words, the digital portrait is what Harun Farocki has called an "operational image", an image that is integrated into a dynamic network in which it has no value other than in terms of the task at hand[86].

The Ambiguous Grid

This journey through the history, rhetoric, and practices of the grid has revealed its incredibly varied functions, uses and meanings. As an aesthetic form, an architectural structure, a graphic tool, an anthropological inventory, a reproduction device and even a computer matrix, the grid is omnipresent in our lives, and precisely because it is ambiguous, both simple and complex, open and closed, limited and infinite,

85 Michael Ensdorf in VON AMELUNXEN, Hubertus et al. (ed.), *Photography After Photography: Memory and Representation in the Digital Age*, London, G&B Arts International, 1997, p. 167.

86 FAROCKI, Harun, "Phantom Images", *Public* 29, 2004, p. 17.

centripetal and centrifugal. Ultimately, this ambiguity, combined with its diversity and ubiquity, seems to be the reason why artists are massively interested in the grid. Whether it is tugged between formal rationalism and spiritual symbolism (Mondrian, Malevitch), objective materialism and subjective sensitivity (Martin), mathematical calculation and random principle (Bill, Molnár, Morellet), serial structure and means of communication (Bochner, LeWitt), scientific tool and performative device (Graham, Antin, Pane), or anonymous inventory and contemplative memorial (Boltanski, Ensdorf), the grid is both the object and the means of artistic criticism. This paradoxical nature is nowhere more apparent than in Rosemarie Trockel's knitted paintings of the 1980s. In *Untitled* [cat., p. 84] (1985), the rose motif spans the entire surface in the manner of Andy Warhol's screen-printed pieces. But in substituting knitted wool for mechanical screen-printing and the sensual motif of the rose for images drawn from the mass media, Trockel delivers an ironic commentary on Pop Art and the mass media as male dominated realms by opposing them to female practices and objects. The background of the image, consisting of a white square and a black square, evokes another adventure in modern art, Malevich's Suprematism. The latter's abstract universalism is also countered by the sensuality of roses and the materiality of wool. "Thinking of textiles as a model for the grid is something of an oxymoron," writes Lucile Encrevé. Indeed, the mathematical, analytical and intellectual nature of the modernist grid – deemed masculine – is in stark contrast to the tangible sensation of textiles, which are still often associated with feminine decorative practices[87]. In Trockel's work, however, these two poles are not mutually exclusive. By superimposing seemingly contradictory approaches, the artist has created a palimpsest where the different layers mutually interact to form a meta-grid, a kind of 'nesting' where one grid displays another grid[88]. Artist Patrick Ireland perfectly summarises the ambiguous nature of the grid: "[The grid] is supposed to be indexical of all that is rational, but I think it's as mad as many logical things turn out to be – artificial, hysterical, subsuming its own version of chaos. It's rigid but flexible, a measure of scale but scaleless, it's flat with imitations of depth, democratic about space but really absolutist, stamped with rigidity but alert with permutational virtuosity. It's a container that contains itself, that is both form and content.[89]"

87 Encrevé, Lucile, "Le textile derrière la grille : une abstraction impure ?", *Perspective. Actualité en histoire de l'art* n° 1, 2016, p. 204. https://journals.openedition.org/perspective/6440, consulted on 18 March 2023.

88 I am referring here to W. J. T. Mitchell. Mitchell's concept of metapicture. *W. J. T. Mitchell, Iconologie: image, texte, idéologie*, Paris, Les Praires ordinaires, 2009, p. 23-24.

89 Ireland, Patrick, *Language Performed / Matters of Identity*, Derry, Orchard Gallery, 1986, p. 21.

Olivia Ardui

"BRAZILIAN GEOMETRY"

The Grid in Contemporary Brazilian Art:
Territories, Identities, and Historical Narratives Under Scrutiny

As a structure formed by the regular intersection of vertical and horizontal lines building up a plane-surface, the grid has been positioned as an emblem of artistic modernity in Euro-American historiography. According to Rosalind Krauss in her seminal 1979 article entitled "Grids", the formal rigour, the mathematical precision, and the regular organisation of this structure states the autonomy of art in the context of the European avant-gardes in the early 20th century. Using a teleological dramaturgy, she associates the resurgence of the grid as a pattern and compositional principle in the works of American artists in the 1950s and 60s to the consecration of art as a pure visuality that was "anti-natural, anti-mimetic, anti-real[1]". Many writers and artists have since exposed the fragility and limitations of these "myths of the avant-garde". And yet the grid and its so-called modernity remain leitmotifs when we consider geometric abstraction, works featuring interlaced lattices or repeated modules, organized following a serial-based logic, up to its reminiscences in contemporary art[2].

Beyond such aesthetic considerations, defining modernity is crucial when addressing its so-called emblem. While Western art is often the reference and starting point of Modernist narratives, to what extent is it possible to address the concept of the grid

1   KRAUSS, Rosalind, "Grids", *October*, Summer 1979, vol. 9, p. 50-64/p. 50. Alexander Streitberger's text featured in this catalogue explores the concept of the grid and its various theoretical applications in more detail.

2   To cite just a few examples: Megan A. Sullivan offers an analysis of the work of Joachim Torres-Garcia using the grid in Megan A. Sullivan, *Radical Form. Modernist Abstraction in South America*, New Haven/London, Yale University Press, 2022 ; CABÑAS, Kaira M., "If the Grid is the New Palm Tree of Latin American Art", *Oxford Art Journal*, vol. 33, n.3, October 2010, p. 365-383; and the recent exhibitions *The Grid in Modern Latin American Art* at Houston's Sicardi Gallery (1 December 2020 – 16 January 2021) or *Grid*, solo exhibition by Ascânio MMM at the Museo Oscar Niemeyer, Curitiba (7 July 2022 – 29 January 2023).

3 Megan A. Sullivan tackles this historiographical turning point in the introduction to her book *Radical Form. Modernist Abstraction in South America, op. cit.* See also MITTER, Partha, "Decentering Modernism: Art History and Avant-Garde Art from the Periphery", *Art Bulletin*, 90, December 2008, p.531-548.

4 Brazil's self-proclaimed modernity is articulated in two phases: on the one hand, the creation of a movement articulated around the concept of anthropophagy in the wake of the 1922 Modern Art Week, which aimed at assimilating the European avant-garde's developments into a figurative style with a national identity in the 1920s; and on the other, the emergence of concretism and universalist abstract language in the 1950s. – DE BELLUZZO, Ana Maria, BANDEIRA, João, BURTON, Victor and MAMMI, Lorenzo, *Brazil.Brasil* (pub.), cat., Brussels, Palais des Beaux-Arts, 4 October 2011 – 15 January 2012, Bruxelles/Anvers, Ludion, 2011.

5 CHAROUX, Lothar, CORDEIRO, Waldemar, DE BARROS, Geraldo, FÉJER, Kazer, HAAR, Leopoldo, SACILOTTO, Luiz and WLADYSLAW, Anatol, "Ruptura", 1952. Manifestoes. Adolpho Leirner Archives at the Museum of Fine Arts, Houston, in International Center for the Arts of the Americas at the Museum of Fine Arts, Houston. Documents of Latin American Art and Latino Art, [https://icaa.mfah.org/s/en/item/771349#?c=&m=&s=&cv=&xywh=-1345%2C-1%2C4288%2C2400], (10/03/23).

6 The rise of these concretist movements has often been compared with the growth of the European avant-garde, particularly the work of Piet Mondrian and Theo van Doesburg, but also with the concretism of the Ulm school in Switzerland, centred around the figure of Max Bill.
NEUBAEUER DA SILVA, Paula Carolina, *A vocação construtiva na arte Sul-americana. Os cinéticos Venezuelanos e os concretos paulistas*, São Paulo, Editora UNESP, 2012 ; BRITO, Ronaldo, "Fluid Geometry", in Ronaldo Brito, Guilherme Bueno and Sonia Salcedo (éds.), *Art in Brazil. 1950 – 2011*, cat., Palais des Beaux-arts, Brussels, 12 octobre 2011 – 15 janvier 2012, Ludion, Anvers, 2011, p. 17-26.

when considering art of the "Global South"? Can we transpose this theoretical framework and narrative scheme to art that is still regarded as peripheral[3]? The question proves particularly relevant when we consider the prominence of abstract-geometric movements in Latin America – and namely in Brazil – in a direct dialogue with the European avant-gardes that Krauss addresses.

This essay explores the grid in contemporary Brazilian art. We will evoke some of the resonances, implications, and specific meanings that this organisational motif and principle can assume in a country that is continually haunted by the spectre of order and progress. Instead of undertaking an exhaustive, cross-disciplinary study of the use of the grid in Brazilian art, we shall examine artworks that appropriate and subvert its logic in conventional images and representations that pervade the country's visual culture: geopolitical maps, illustrations by European travellers, *azulejo* mural decorations or even ethno-racial taxonomies and classification systems. We hope to demonstrate that these diverse ways of materialising the grid questions the understanding of (artistic) modernity in a territory marked by (neo)colonial greed, constant conflict, political instability and acute social, economic, and racial inequalities.

The Grid as a Pilot Plan for Modernity?

Before examining the work of contemporary artists, we'll briefly look back at the emergence of concretism in Brazil in the 1950s – a foundational moment in the construction of Brazilian identity. With the advent of a universal abstract language, somehow freed from narrative and mimetic imperatives, concretism became synonymous with the country's modernity and modernisation, a sort of point zero and rupture with the past[4]. This clear distinction between the "old" and the "new" was envisioned in 1952 by the *Grupo Ruptura* of São Paulo concrete artists led by Waldemar Cordeiro [Fig. 1]. In its manifesto, the Group stated its categorical opposition not only to "all varieties and hybrids of naturalism", but also to "hedonic non-figuration, a product of gratuitous taste, aimed solely at arousing pleasure or displeasure[5]". This new aesthetic advocates a revival of the "essential values of visual art", which translates into a rational, logical and methodical approach based on the rigorous arrangement of repetitive lines, modules and geometric motifs – a movement that could thus perfectly fit into Krauss's formalist genealogy of the grid[6].

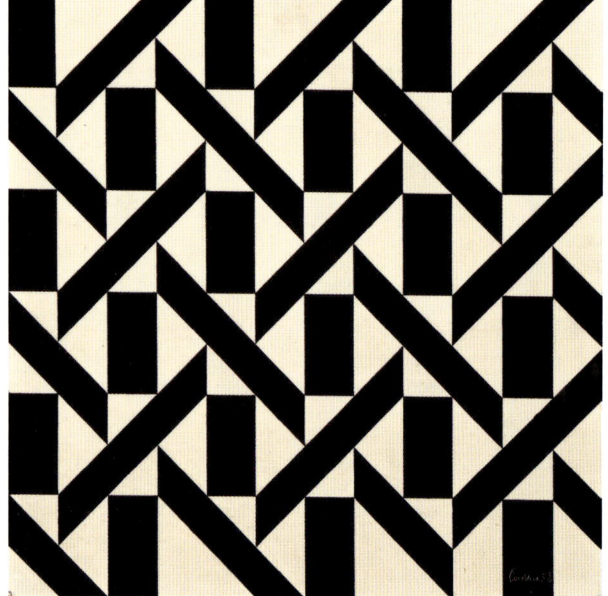

Fig. 1

Waldemar Cordeiro
Sem Titulo, 1958
Enamel on particle board, 52.3 × 52.2 cm
Collection of Hecilda and Sergio Fadel

A few years later, the manifesto of Concrete Poetry introduced an overlapping between formal research and programmatic urban planning, between graphic and geopolitical space. The *Projeto Piloto para a poesia concreta* [Pilot Plan for Concrete Poetry] was published in March 1958 in issue 4 of the magazine *Noigandres* – the name of the eponymous group formed by Décio Pignatari and brothers Augusto and Haroldo de Campos. In this text, the authors formulated their aesthetic position, arguing for an experimental form of poetry that would explore the rhythmic and sonic qualities of words, and the importance of their composition and placement on the page. This now "spatial or visual syntax", in which "graphic space [is] the structural agent" [7], reverberates beyond the confines of the blank page. In fact, the title *plano piloto* [pilot plan] refers to Lúcio Costa's urban planning project for Brasília. Shortlisted as part of a national competition he had won the previous year, Costa's design proposed a schematic structuring of the city, which would be set in the equivalent of the country's geographical centre, articulated around two monumental orthogonal axes, and split into sectors of activity grouped in the same areas (residential, recreational, or working areas). By establishing this connection between urban and artistic projection,

7   DE CAMPOS, Augusto, PIGNATARI, Décio and DE CAMPOS, Haroldo, "Plano-pilôto para poesia concreta" [Pilot Plan for Concrete Poetry] (1958), in Mary Ellen Solt, *Concrete Poetry: A World View*, Bloomington, Indiana University Press, 1970, p. 71–72. KHOURI, Omar, "Noigandres e invenção. Revistas porta-vozes da Poesia Concreta", *Facom*, n.16, 2006, p. 26 [https://www.faap.br/revista_faap/revista_facom/facom_16/omar.pdf].

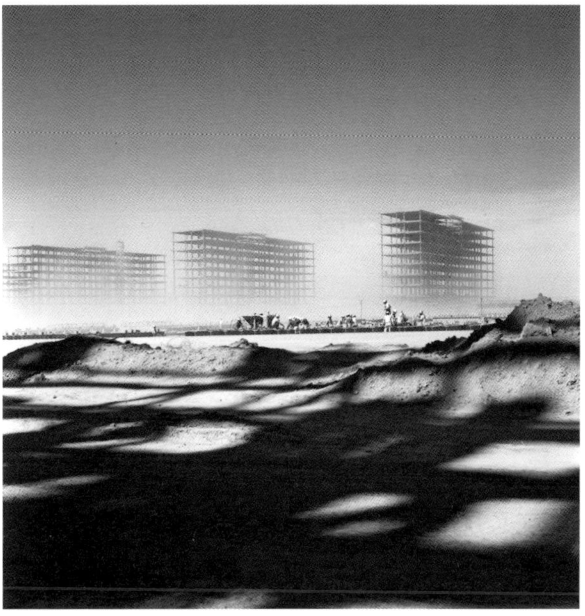

Noigandres' ambitions are clearly expressed: epitomising modernity just as the monumental and Cartesian utopia of the country's new capital.

The construction of Brasilia [Fig. 2] mirrors a period of accelerated economic growth, urbanisation, and industrialisation that started in the 1940s. These were years brimming with optimism, prosperity, and a desire to establish the country as an active player on the international stage. In parallel, a large-scale cultural project celebrated abstraction and geometric formalism as emblems of this development, which was quickly appropriated and propagated by the state, but also backed to a large extent by private funding[8]. In this context, major new institutions were established progressively installed into the new buildings designed by modernist architects like Oscar Niemeyer. These new exhibition venues played a crucial role in spreading the influence of concretism: the Museums of Modern Art in Rio de Janeiro and São Paulo in 1948, the São Paulo Museum of Art in 1949 and, of course, the São Paulo Biennial in 1951 – a prime example of the political recuperation of abstract visuality in Latin America[9]. It is no coincidence, moreover, that Max Bill – and *in extenso* the

8 SULLIVAN, Megan A., *op. cit.*, p. 15.

9 *Ibid.*

aesthetic of concretism that he embodies – was awarded the first prize for sculpture at the inaugural edition of the São Paulo Biennial, and would have a profound impact on the local art scene.

But more than simply emulating and assimilating European modernist artistic models, Brazil's rejection of a mimetic narrative goes well beyond the aesthetic. According to Ronaldo Brito, in a nation-state born out of an empirical colonial process that prioritised the exploitation of land and resources over systematic planning, the constructive momentum – in the broadest sense of the term – brought with it a sense of freedom and emancipation. The advent of geometric formalism and large-scale spatial planning can be interpreted as two facets of a doctrine of programmes aimed at breaking with the supposedly bygone past[10]. This confidence in progress, incarnated in constructive thinking applied to art, architecture, and space, quickly faded in the years that followed, particularly in the wake of the military dictatorship (1964-1985). The grid came to be used as a model against which artists problematised notions of territory and national identity, namely through the use and appropriation of cartographic imagery[11].

The Cartographic Grid

Cildo Meireles's *Arte física* [Physical Art] is a series of poetic and performative pieces subverting the operations of locating coordinates in space and delimiting borders or geolocated areas. *Arte física: Caixas de Brasília / Clareira* [Physical Art: Brasilia Boxes/Clearing] (1969) [Fig. 3] stems from an action to demarcate and explore the territory of the new capital. Wooden steles linked by ropes mark out an orthogonal area on the banks of Lake Paranoá. The accumulation of excavated soil is burnt in the centre of the area; its ashes placed inside a first box, which is then buried on the site. Some of the remaining earth is then placed in a second and third box, where the remnants of the fire, wooden steles, and ropes are also kept. The reminiscences of this performance are assembled in an installation that includes the two boxes, a map of Brasilia locating the scene of the action, and photographic documentation organized sequentially in a grid. As Meireles explains, the motivation for this intervention was to take possession of the site and establish

Cildo Meireles
Arte física: Caixas de Brasília / Clareira, 1969
Photographs, map, wooden boxes, installation
of variable dimensions
© Cildo Meireles / Tate. Photo Pat Kilgore

Cildo Meireles
Arte física: Marco Tordesilhas, 1969
Indian ink, graphite and collage
on graph paper, 32 × 45 cm
© Cildo Meireles / Tate. Photo Pat Kilgore

10 Brito, Ronaldo, "Fluid Geometry", in Ronaldo Brito, Guilherme Bueno and Sonia Salcedo (pub.), *Art in Brazil. 1950 – 2011*, cat., Palais des Beaux-Arts, Brussels, 12 October 2011 – 15 January 2012, Ludion, Anvers, 2011, p. 17.

11 Elena Shtromberg points to the recurrence of cartography in Brazilian art, and associates it with three contextual elements that have a crucial impact on the conceptualisation of space: the construction of Brasilia between 1957 and 1960, the landing on the Moon in 1969, which had a lasting effect on the way we understand navigation and perspective, and, finally, the mass displacement of indigenous communities in the Amazon by military government initiatives such as the construction of the Trans-Amazonian Highway in 1972. Cf.: Shtromberg, Elena, *Art systems in Brazil & the 1970s*, Austin, University of Texas Press, 2016, p. 11; 123.

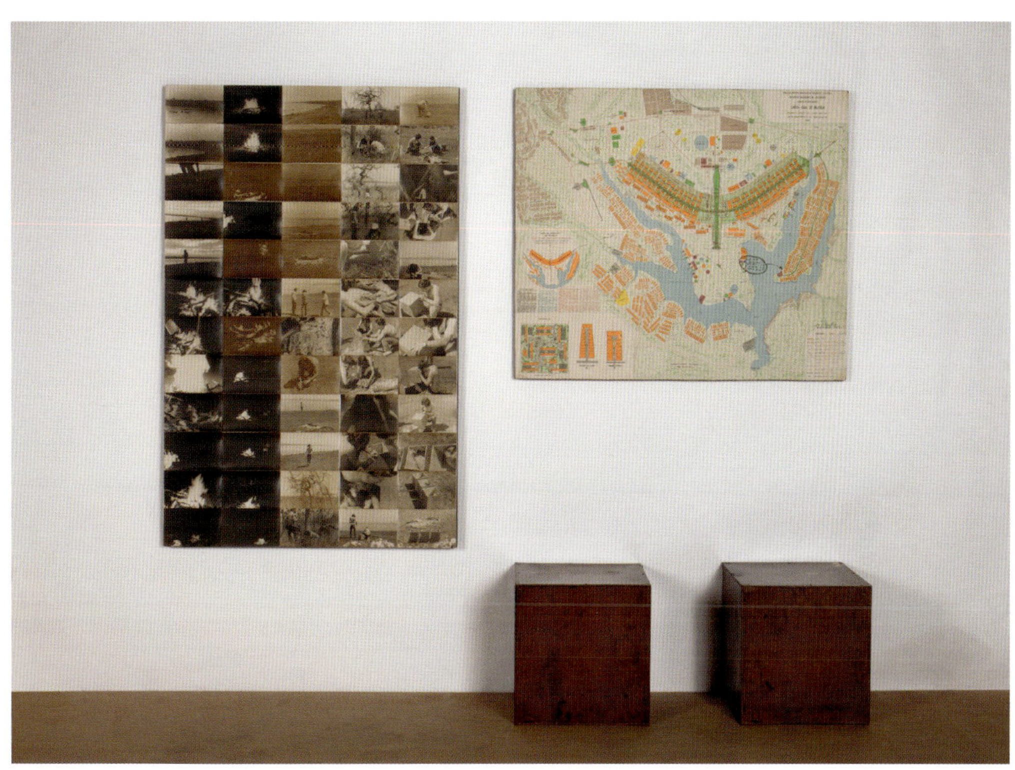

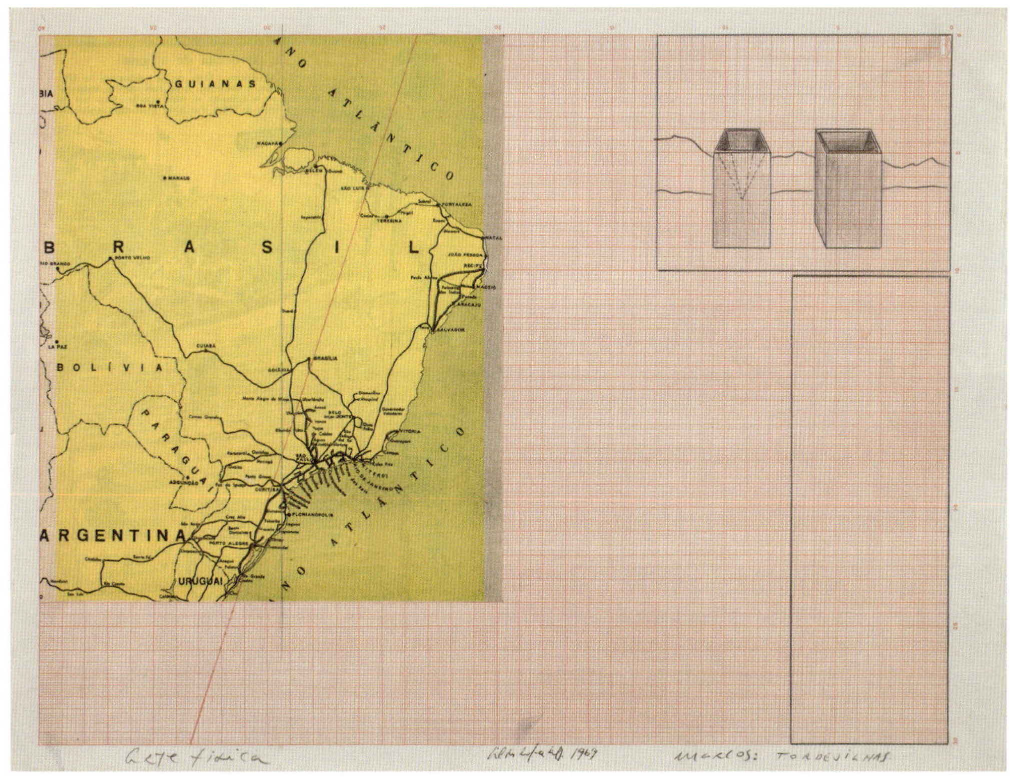

a "free territory" in Brasília, the seat of political power structured and armoured by the modernist urban grid. This action seemed particularly controversial in the context of a military regime, and police officers visited the site to surveil closely the suspicious operation[12].

While other interventions in the series were never completed, they remain as drawings and notes reflecting improbable, even fanciful purposes defined by the artist –measuring fleeting atmospheric phenomena (linking the two starting points of a rainbow), containing moving fluids (the falling points of a waterfall) – or pertaining to speculative fiction (sailing in the opposite direction to the earth's rotation in order to get younger). Ironically, these potential interventions – a kind of "conceptual land art" to use the words of critic Gerardo Mosquera[13] – are materialized as collages and drawings on graph paper, which is the medium of choice for engineering and architectural projects. For *Arte física: Marco Tordesilhas* [Physical Art: Tordesilhas] (1969) [Fig. 4], Meireles intended to stretch a rope from Laguna – in the south of the country – to the Amazon, shifting the border defined by the Treaty of Tordesilhas in 1494 by a few degrees. This imaginary line divided the world between the Portuguese and the Spanish during the great invasions of the 15th and 16th centuries as a graphic manifestation of colonial covetousness[14].

The arbitrality of cartographic grids is also challenged by Anna Bella Geiger, an artist who has systematically appropriated planispheres since the 1970s. In her series *Fronteiriçios* [Borderlines] for example, the artist uses archive drawers covered with a layer of wax, on which metal sheets are arranged following the lines of geopolitical borders. In *Local da ação com Euhropa/Bras. AM. LAT.* [Place of Action with Euhropa/Bras. LAT. AM.] [Fig. 5], the territories of Brazil and Latin America are silhouetted side by side, while wires positioned orthogonally form a grid reminiscent of a map of the world, with the exception that some of the wires are loose, twisted, or broken. By altering the rigidity and orthogonality of this lattice, Geiger suggests – just like Meirelles in *Arte física: Marco Tordesilhas* – conceivable breaks in the structure of restraint and control embodied by the grid. The artist's interest in maps resides precisely in the possibility of "subverting their descriptive meanings [and highlighting their] ideological implications by altering certain scales and proportions through the use of distortions.[15]"

12 REBOUÇAS, Júlia and MATOS, Diego, *Cildo Meireles. Entrevendo*, cat., SESC-Pompéia, São Paulo, 26 September 2019 – 2 February 2020, São Paulo, SESC-SP, 2019, p. 54-55.

13 MOSQUERA, Gerardo and MEIRELES, Cildo, "In conversation", in Paulo Herkenhoff, Gerardo Mosquera and Dan Cameron, *Cildo Meireles*, Phaidon, London, 1999, p. 29.

14 MATOS, Diego, "A natureza do espaço brasileiro. Entrevista Cildo Meireles", *América – revista da pós-graduação da escola da cidade*, n., 2020, p. 14. MATOS, Diego, *Cildo Meireles – Espaço, modos de usar*, doctoral thesis submitted to the University of Saõ Paulo, Faculty of Architecture and Urban Planning, (Agnaldo Farias, promoter), 2014, p. 111.

15 Anna Bella Geiger, cited in TOLEDO, Tomás, "Viscera, Maps and Portraits", in Adriano Pedrosa and Tomás Toledo, *Anna Bella Geiger*, cat., São Paulo, MASP, 29 November 2019 – 1 mars 2020/Ghent, S.M.A.K., 29 May – 11 October 2020, São Paulo, MASP, 2019, p. 33.

Anna Bella Geiger
Local da ação com Euhropa / Bras. AM. LAT.,
série *Fronteiriços,* 1995

Iron drawer, encaustic and copper wire,
35 × 63 × 10.5 cm
Artist's collection, Rio de Janeiro

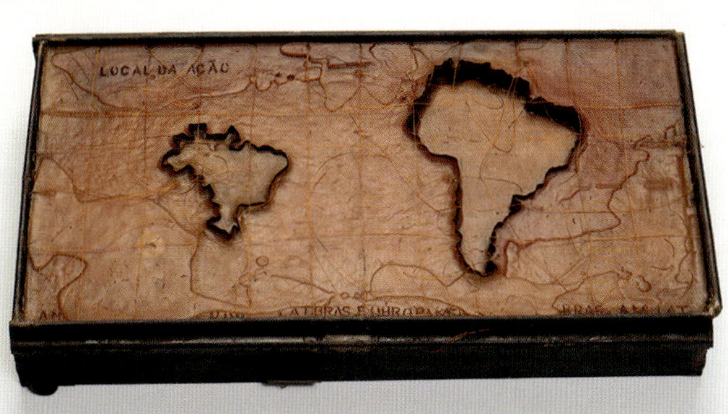

Picturesque vs Alien

In *Brasil nativo/Brasil alienigena* [Native Brazil/Alien Brazil] (1976-77) [Fig. 6], Geiger indirectly refers to another type of conventional and documentary image that widely circulated in Brazil: the many illustrations by European travelling artists. Here, the Geiger uses a grid layout with two rows of postcards facing each other. One row shows staged images of the Bororo indigenous individuals in their so-called autochthone setting, while the other images depict the artist in an urban context, albeit in similar postures and actions. The type of postcards in the first row were very much in vogue in the 1970s, and could be bought in newsagents. The native populations were depicted dancing, shooting arrows with their bows, and sweeping the space in front of a hut in settlements or in the jungle, contributing to reinforce clichés about these native populations represented and regarded as "primitive" in comparison with "modern" city dwellers. Such an idealised, non-confrontational vision of the "native" recalls the typology employed in the illustrations of travelling artists such as Jean-Baptiste Debret in his *Voyage pittoresque et historique*

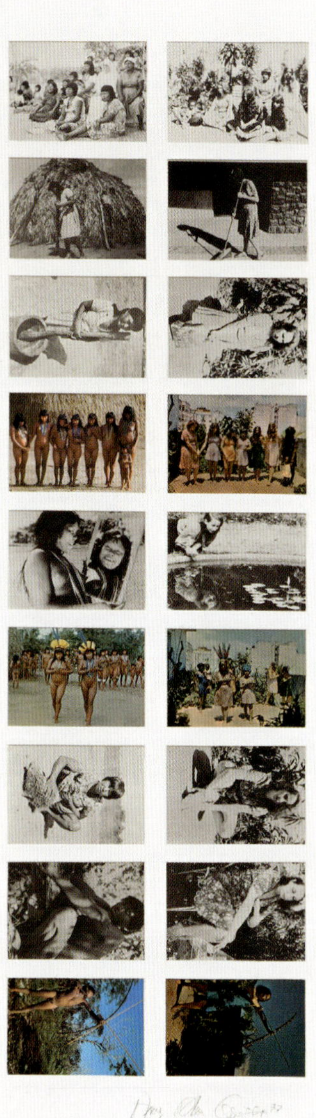

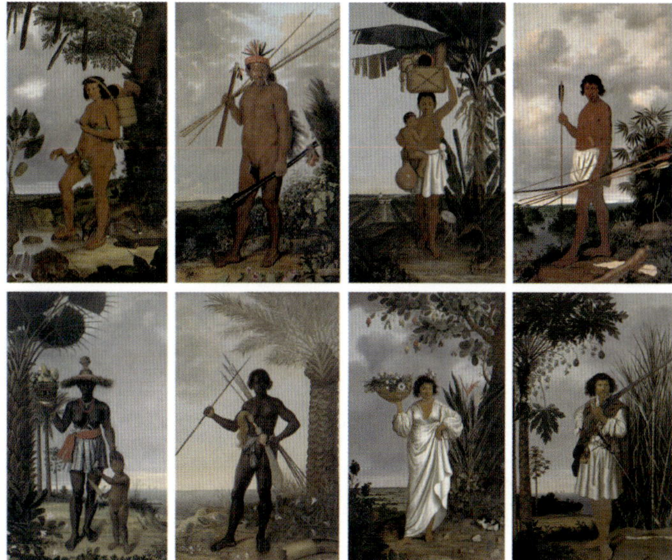

16 Aucardo Chicangana-Bayona, Yobenj,
"Os Tupis e os Tapuias de Eckhout:
O declínio da imagem renascentista do
índio", *VARIA HISTORIA*, vol. 24, nº 40,
2008, p. 539.

17 Brett, Guy, "Para Anna Bella Geiger",
in Adolfo Montejo Navas, *Anna Bella
Geiger: Territórios Passagens Situações*,
Rio de Janeiro, Casa da Palavra, 2007,
p. 46.

au Brésil (1834-37) and Albert Eckhout's series of paintings of typological pairs [Fig. 7].

Having joined the Dutch mission in Brazil between 1637 and 1644, Albert Eckhout was the first to depict native populations in life-size paintings. The series consists of pairs of men and women from the same ethnic group and distinguishes between more or less "civilised" groups, based largely on their attire. At the time, these images widely circulated and were reproduced in a variety of media, including Zacharias Wagenaer's engravings (1637-1641)[16]. The development of a common imaginary and its dissemination echoes the postcards used in Geiger's work. The broad circulation of staged images proved a perverse strategy for winning over public opinion as major roads were being laid through the Amazon in the 1970s. The purpose was to intentionally conceal and obscure the violence of the urbanisation process and exploitation of indigenous land, so as to cover up the violent side-effects of the alleged developmental progress during the period of the military dictatorship[17].

By re-enacting and parodying these postcards, Geiger demonstrates the fictional and artificial dimension of these scenes which, like world maps and other traditional representations, served economic and political interests and motives. The way in which the postcards are arranged – facing one another – prompts a comparative reading reminiscent of Eckhout's typological pairs. But "with [her] lack of preparation as a primitive man" – a maxim that subtitles the work and appears on the back of each postcard – Geiger ridicules and dismisses the binary "civilised-savage" divide emerging from a simplistic confrontation between the Bororo individuals and a white, Polish woman. Embodying and opposing the picturesque "native Brazil" with the "alien Brazil", these *tableaux vivants* pose the complex construct of Brazilian identity, resisting linear schemes hinged on crude dichotomies between past and present, "civilised" and "native".

The Azulejo Grid

"Racial democracy" – a watered-down version of the colonial process and the original myth of authentic Brazilian identity – refers to the illusion of peaceful and harmonious coexistence between races – whites, blacks, and "natives" – to use the title of Geiger's work[18]. Adriana Varejão is an artist who problematises this concept through the use of a recurring grid structure in architecture: *azulejos*, Portuguese wall decorations formed by a series of painted ceramic tiles placed side by side. In *Azulejaria em Carne Viva* [Tilework in Live Flesh] [Fig. 8], the surface of the painting simulates a wall covered in *azulejos* with floral and plant motifs laid out in a regular, squared-off, repetitive composition. With its stylised decoration, this modular surface, reminiscent of a section of wall of a colonial baroque building, is shredded and flayed by an eruption of shapeless bowels under its two-dimensional surface. The grid-surface incarnating the imported Portuguese visual and cultural model is perforated by a mass of disembowelled entrails of unidentifiable eviscerated bodies. Rendered with brilliant illusionism, the piece embodies the horror of the carnage perpetrated during the invasion and colonisation of Brazil and serves as a reminder of the brutality and hypocrisy of the pacifist rhetoric that continues to permeate the country's collective imagination[19].

Varejão's use of azulejos does not only refer to the colonial period, but also to its modernist reinterpretation. One example is *Azulejões* [Fig. 9], a monumental installation made up of modular canvases juxtaposed with sections of rocaille motifs,

18 FREYRE, Gilberto, *Casa Grande e Senzala*, Rio de Janeiro, Maia & Schmidt, 1934.
For more information on racial issues in Brazil from a historical perspective, see: MORITZ SCHWARTCZ, Lilia, *O Espeáculo das Raças: cientistas, instituições e questão racial no Brasil (1870-1930)*, São Paulo, Companhia das Letras, 1993.

19 GODFREY, Tony, *La peinture aujourd'hui*, New York, Phaidon, 2010, p. 279-280. DOROSHENKO, Peter, "Adriana Varejão", in *Nouvelles perspectives en peinture*, New York, Phaidon, 2003, p. 336.

Adriana Varejão
Azulejaria de tapete em carne viva, 1999
Oil, foam, wood, aluminium and canvas,
150 × 190 × 25 cm
Courtsesy of the artist. Photo Vicente de Mello

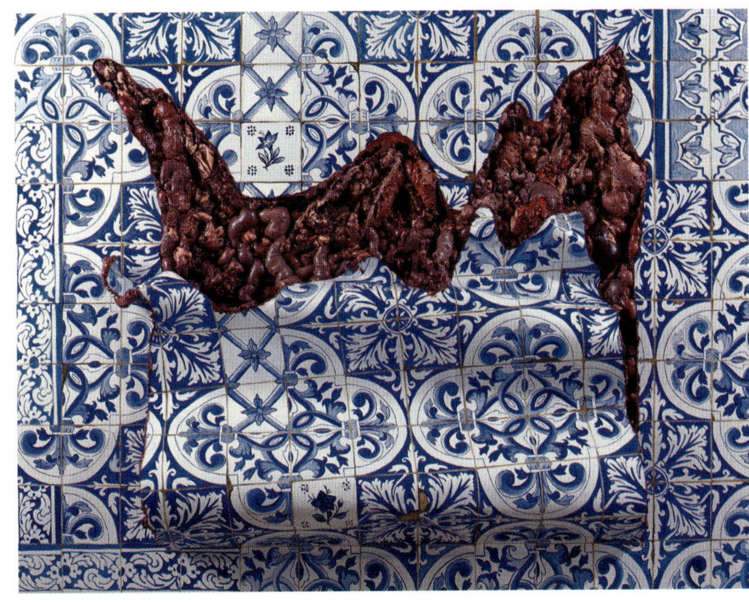

but arranged in a random, discontinuous order. In this piece, each tile represents a fraction of an ornament that is so prevalent in the decoration of Baroque buildings in Brazil. When put together, the pieces emerge as a fragmented cacophony. Paulo Herkenhoff suggests a parallel between the irregular arrangement of the different modules in the grid of tiles and Athos Bulcão's *modus operandi*. Having created a number of tiled walls with simple geometric motifs, the artist has been instrumental in reviving the medium, conjuring up the historical tradition of *azulejos* while simultaneously introducing a modernist visuality integrated into architecture, most notably in Oscar Niemeyer's Brasilia buildings. Bulcão has often relinquished the decision on how to orientate these modular tiles to the project managers, relying on a formal game with a few rules, such as respect for orthogonality and serialism[20].

"To fully understand the cultural fabric within which [Varejão] operates," explains Herkenhoff, "we must remember that the tradition of using tiles in architecture was revived in Brazil in the 1930s. Lúcio Costa, the man primarily credited with incorporating this art form into construction, was at the forefront of this practice [...] In those days, Modernism did not shy away

20 Herkenhoff, Paulo, "glória!, o grande caldo" in *Adriana Varejão*, São Paulo, Takano Editora Gráfica, 2001», [http://www.adrianavarejao.net/media/textos/herkenhof_gloria.pdf], p. 2.

Fig. 9

Adriana Varejão
Azulejões (instalação Itaubanco, SP), 2000
Oil and plaster on canvas, installation made up of 27 paintings,
27 × (100 × 100 cm)
Courtsesy of the artist. Photo Sergio Guerini

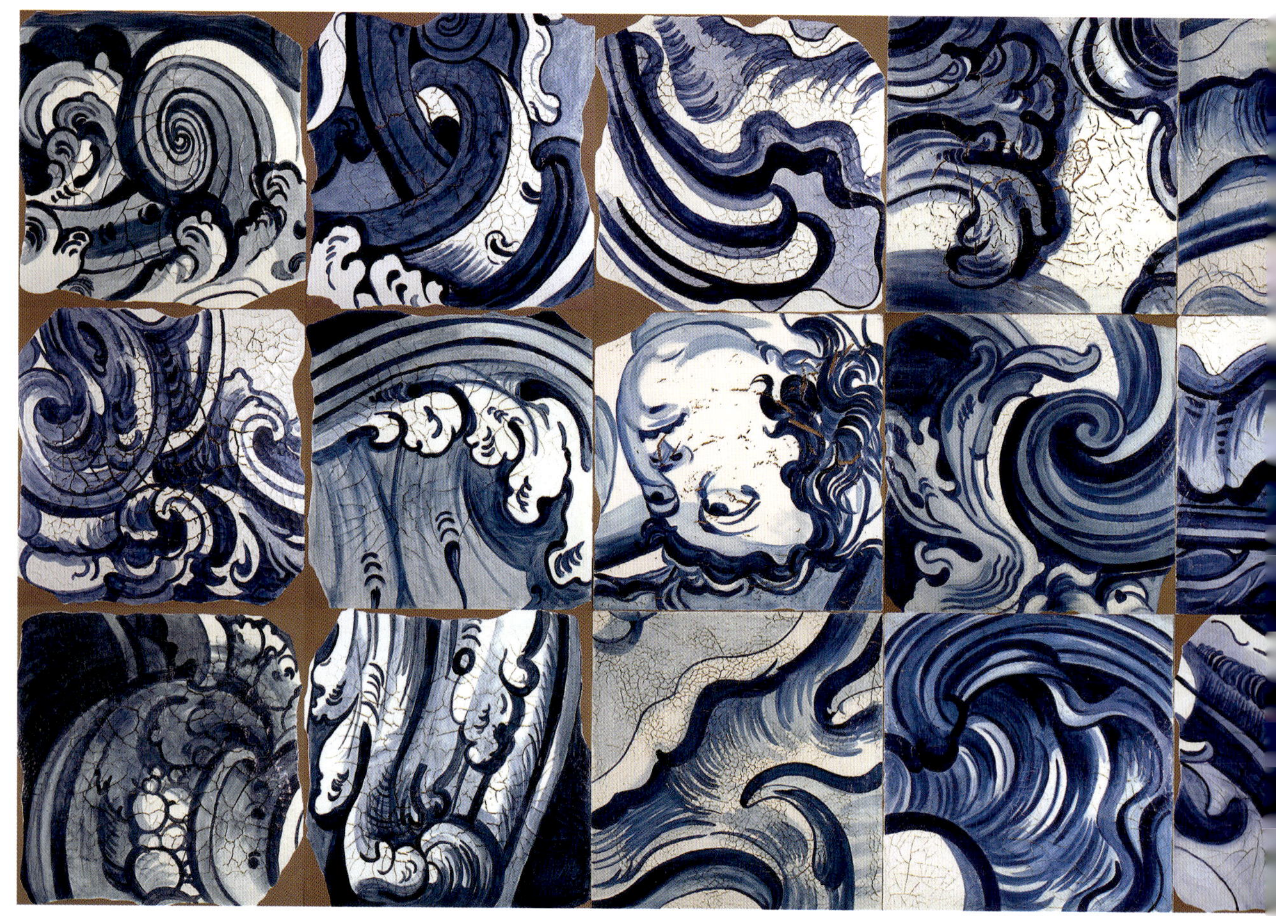

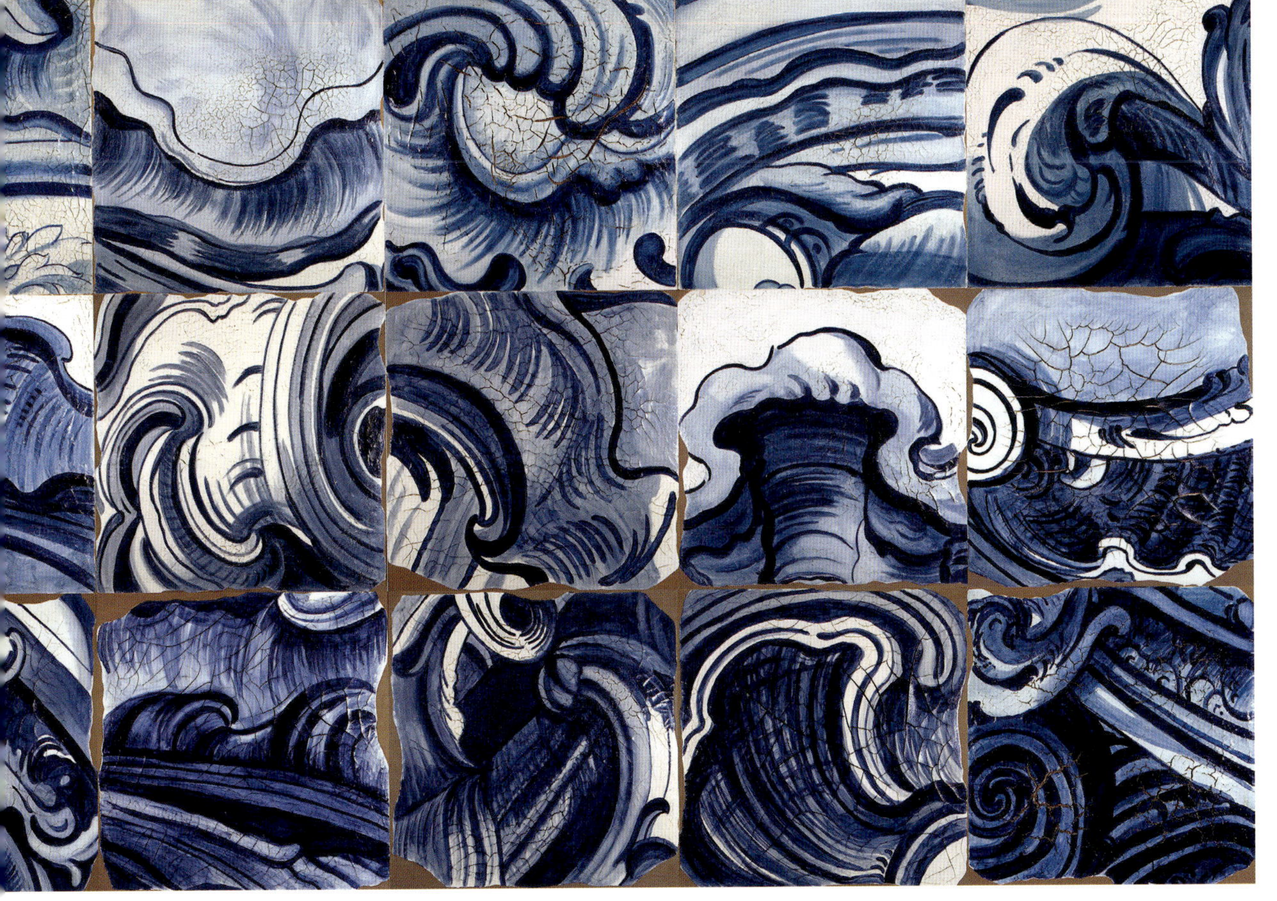

from reclaiming its cultural past as a means of projecting its future and its identity as a country[21]". Thus, the suggestion of the regular structure of *azulejos* and their random, non-continuous placement inside a compositional grid can be read as a uniquely relevant strategy for revisiting colonial visuality and its survival in the modernist utopias.

The Taxonomic Grid

In Rosana Paulino's *A geometria à brasileira chega ao paraíso tropical* [Brazilian Geometry arrives in tropical paradise] (2018) [Fig. 10], colonial imagery is once again superimposed on the utopic projections of abstraction. This series of collages on paper feature different geometric shapes arranged contiguously, overlaid, or covered by photographs of enslaved individuals, craniometric studies, and plates from zoological or botanical textbooks akin to those written by explorer Carl Friedrich Philip von Martius[22]. While without an explicitly drawn or visible grid, the placement of the different images roughly matching the intersections of an invisible lattice brings structure to the composition, anchoring heterogeneous and anachronistic elements in the graphic space of the page. As a result, two periods of the country's history appear to coexist on the same surface. On the one hand, the abstract quadrangular shapes in primary colours allude to the emergence of the concretist movements in the country from the 1950s onwards (the title also suggests that this is a "Brazilian version" of the European modernist avant-garde). On the other hand, the figurative elements of these collages evoke taxonomic and classification systems applied to flora and fauna, but more particularly to enslaved individuals. The artist systematically conceals the faces or eyes of the individuals with geometric shapes, evoking the obliteration of their subjectivities. *A geometria à brasileira chega ao paraíso tropical* suggests that, in the same way as the developmentalist growth of the 1950s, invasion and colonisation are the two sides of a single oppression rooted in the distant horizon of a supposed "civilisation".

Racist iconography, which plays a consistent role in the artist's work, is once again scrutinised through the grid to convey the perversity and violence of the civilisational, rational, and logical precepts that it may have embodied. In *A permanência das estruturas* [The permanence of structures] (2017) [Fig. 11], the logic of collage is applied to textile, with photographs and illustrations printed on fabric panels roughly sewn together like

21 *Ibid.*

22 PICCOLI, Valéria and NERY, Pedro, *Rosana Paulino, a costura da mémoria*, cat., São Paulo, Pinacoteca do Estado, 8 December 2018 – 4 March 2019, São Paulo, Pinacoteca do Estado, 2018, p. 11.

Fig. 10

Rosana Paulino

A geometria à brasileira chega ao paraíso tropical, 2018

Digital print, collage, and monotype on paper,
48 × 33 cm
Courtesy of the Artist and Mendes Wood DM São Paulo,
Brussels, New York
© Rosana Paulino. Photo Isabella Matheus

Fig. 11

Rosana Paulino

A permanência das estruturas, 2017

Digital print on fabric, acrylic paint and stitching,
93 × 110 cm
Courtesy of the Artist and Mendes Wood DM São Paulo,
Brussels, New York
© Rosana Paulino. Photo Isabella Matheus

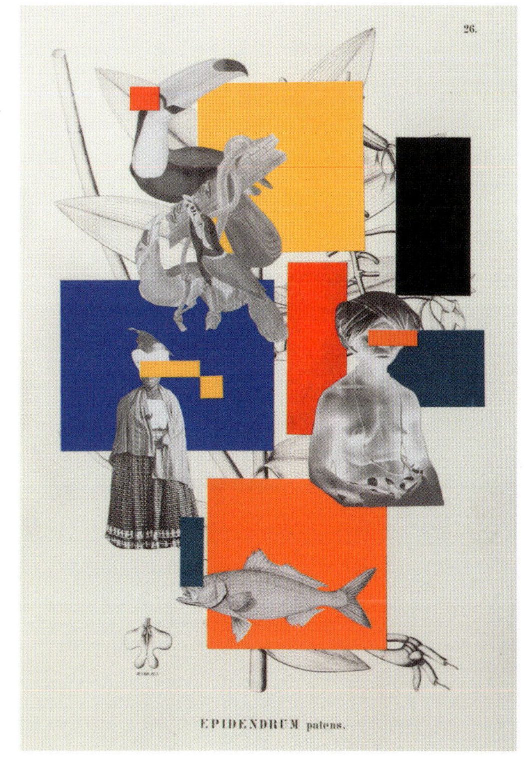

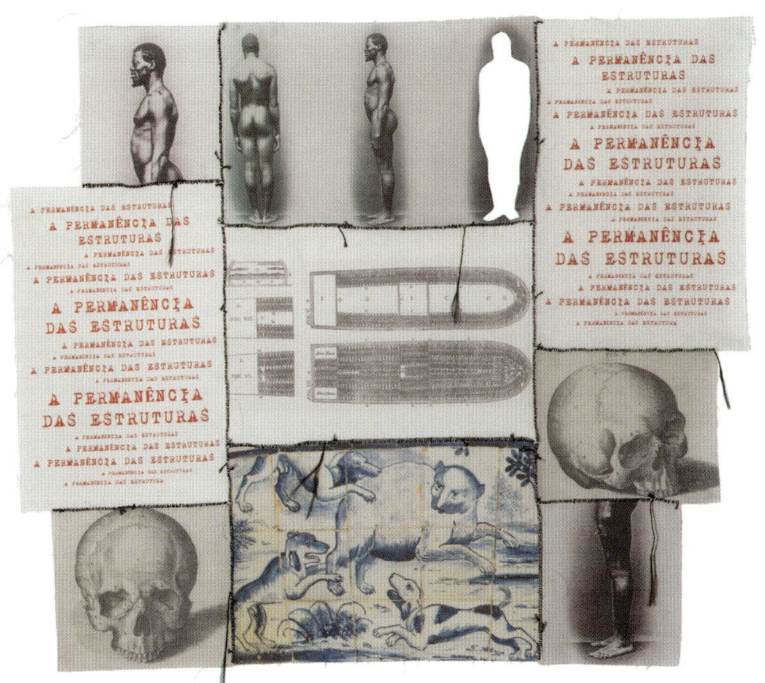

patchwork. The whole is made up of three columns and three rows, once again combining anachronistic images that widely circulated in Brazil and beyond. The central panel is a reproduction of the floor plan and section of a slave ship, which shows the cramped arrangement of enslaved bodies placed side by side in a linear, regular disposition – resembling a grid. The perversity of slavery finds a telling metaphor in the hunting scene depicted in the *azulejo* printed on the lower panel. Invoking the Portuguese tile decorations as an index of colonisation, in a similar way as Varejão had done, the artist explains that "the azulejos representing hunting scenes are the first to appear [...] and give an idea of this predatory dimension of colonisation and, worse still, as if we accepted this predatory dimension, it is maintained aesthetically[23]".

Other panels evoke death, emptiness, and disappearance. Three modules reproduce the ethnographic photographs of an Afro-descendant man shown in profile and from behind by the photographer Auguste Stahl, commissioned by Louis Agassiz, an advocate of racial determinism based on pseudo biological criteria. In the same serial logic as this type of eugenic representation, we can assume that a third view, from the front, existed, but his body was cut out of the textile matrix on which it was printed. All that remains is a negative silhouette, an invisible spectre, perhaps one of many ghosts to have succumbed to the violence of this oppressive system. Illustrations of skulls – commonly used to justify racial theories – are reproduced in modules on both sides of the central panel with the section of the slave ship. Set within this grid-like composition and placed alongside the other images evoking the imminent mortality of the slave trade, the skulls become macabre allegories, a sort of *memento mori* for colonial economics[24].

While the artwork generally adopts a rows-and-columns layout, the strictness of the orthogonal grid is broken by the discontinuity of the horizontal lines, which are slightly offset. Moreover, the junction between the panels is materialised by a coarse seam where the black thread contrasts with the light-coloured fabric on which the images are printed. Amidst the distorted orthogonality of the grid, colonial imagery is correlated to the present. Printed on the two other modules making up the artwork, the title implies that the racism that motivated the production of these images is still very much structurally alive in Brazil. Indeed, the artist explained that the inspiration for the title was sparked by learning of the arbitrary imprisonment of a young racialised man – a recurring scenario in a country

23 Rosana Paulino cited in: HERCI FERREIRA JÚNIOR, Antonio, "Rosana Paulino : colcha de retalhos e sutura da resistência histórica", acts of the XII colloque International Criadores Sobre outras Obras, *A via das máscaras: as artes em Congresso no CSO 2021*, Lisbon, 26 March – 3 April 2021, p. 213.

24 *Ibid.*

where police violence against Afro-Brazilians and social ine-qualities are blatant[25]. While Rosana Paulino acknowledges this ongoing violence, the stitches she employs seem to reflect a necessary elaboration and assimilation of these historical epi-sodes and the open wounds linking them to the present.

While Krauss's conception of the grid finds echoes in the rise of geometric abstraction in Brazil in the 1950s, it would seem that even then, the constructive impetus could not be disasso-ciated from the issues of spatial planning, the shaping of a national identity, and a projection into the future based on a reinterpretation of the past. Instead of a formalist reading of the grid as an emblem of artistic modernity, we have looked at the work of contemporary artists questionning its application to certain conventional representations such as cartography, modular ornamentation, and taxonomy. In this context, the grid functions primarily as a dispositif – whether real or sym-bolic – for controlling and abstractly containing a territory and the subjects who inhabit it. The artworks by Cildo Meireles, Anna Bella Geiger, Adriana Varejão and Rosana Paulino address and reveal the ideological implications of the grid in these ubiquitous images in the country's visual culture, thereby deconstructing, loosening, ripping apart, or stitching together it's sharp-edged sides.

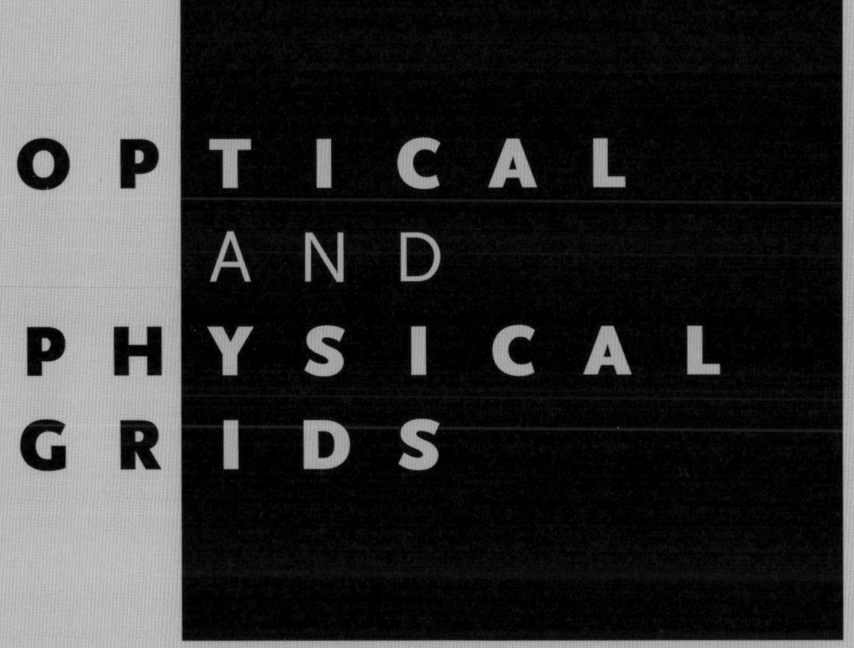

OPTICAL
AND
PHYSICAL
GRIDS

This section starts from the observation made by the American art historian Rosalind Krauss that the grid forms the basis of modernist painting, which emphasises the artistic medium and its optical, tactile and formal qualities. While Piet Mondrian and Theo van Doesburg introduced the grid around 1920 as a rational, abstract system to liberate painting from its mimetic role, the Zurich concrete artists Max Bill, Richard Paul Lohse and Verena Loewensberg adopted it in the 1940s and 1950s as an informational framework capable of producing series, progressions and combinations that would allow art to be conceived as a system of aesthetic communication.

From around 1960 onwards, the artists of GRAV (Groupe de recherche d'art visuel), including François Morellet, Vera Molnár and Jesús Rafael Soto, started to manipulate the rigid armour of the grid by integrating random operations and optical effects (moirés, scintillations, diffraction, interference, etc.) to disrupt perception and challenge the viewer. Along with Michael Noll, Frieder Nake, Georg Nees and Manfred Mohr, Molnár was one of the pioneers of digital or Generative Art. Through the use of computers, these artists create programmed pieces based on algorithmic operations, with "its immense combinatorial capacity to facilitate the systematic investigation of an infinite range of possibilities" (Molnár). The grid morphs into a computer matrix where rational calculation rhymes with subjective imagination.

Throughout the 1960s, cybernetic and systemic theories enjoyed great popularity in the United States, at a time when Minimalism and Conceptual Art were gathering momentum. In opposition to the modernist idea of an autonomous art that only refers to its own creation, artists such as Carl Andre, Sol LeWitt, Dan Graham, and Douglas Huebler adopted the grid to conceptualise the work of art as a serial structure, interacting with its exhibition space and the audience, or as an information system whose elements only have a meaning in relation to the connections they have with each other.

From a post-conceptual, post-modernist perspective, Sherrie Levine and Rosemarie Trockel appropriate the strategies of the artistic avant-gardes to tackle the question of the authenticity and originality of the artwork and to expose the predominantly male character of modern art. Levine's irregular chessboards, which she began painting in the mid-1980s, belied the mathematical nature of constructivist painting and the Surrealists' penchant for games and chance. For her part, Trockel has been making knitted paintings since 1984. Using a practice that is traditionally associated with women, she derides the processes – born of a capitalist and patriarchal system – of industrial mechanical reproduction and the serial repetition of motifs in mass culture as it is celebrated in Pop Art. **AS**

Verena Loewensberg was born in Zurich on 28 May 1912, and died in the same city on 27 April 1986. Together with Max Bill, Richard-Paul Lohse, and Camille Graeser, she was a leading figure of the Zurich Concrete Art movement. Between 1927 and 1929, she studied drawing, weaving, and colour theory at the Basel School of Applied Arts. In the 1930s, she began creating constructive works on paper. During this period, she discovered the Abstraction-Création group thanks to Max Bill. She also met Theo van Doesburg and Georges Vantongerloo, both of whom had a major influence on her work. In 1936, she took part in *Zeitprobleme in der Schweizer Malerei und Plastik (Problems of our times in Swiss Painting and Sculpture)* at the Kunsthaus in Zurich, an exhibition that proved decisive in the emergence of Concrete Art in Switzerland.

Following a period of experimentation in the 1930s and 1940s and under the influence of De Stijl and Constructivism, Loewensberg developed her own style from 1950 onwards, using bold colours, combining primary and intermediate tones, and rhythmically arranging lines, circles, triangles, and squares, often according to the principles of rotation and progression. Unlike other members of the Zurich Concrete Art movement, Loewensberg favoured intuition, poetry and psychic energy to counterbalance the mathematical, rational character of her compositions. "I don't have a theory, I just follow what comes into my head", she declared in 1977. From 1966 onwards, she produced a series of assemblages and cycles of works focusing on variations in geometric shapes and colour tones, which she then arranged intuitively to create a lyrical atmosphere. Printing techniques became particularly important as she explored new formal and thematic ideas. An avid music lover, jazz had a profound influence on her artistic work. We might compare the repetitive use of her visual vocabulary with the *riff* – a short melodic motif repeated rhythmically in a loop – and the geometric organisation of her compositions with the *chord grid*, a musical notation system composed of boxes containing harmonic and rhythmic information to accompany a melody.

Untitled, a silkscreen print from 1976, is a musically inspired work in this vein. Sixty-six squares are arranged across the

Verena Loewensberg
Untitled, 1976

surface, forming part of a modular system based on a grid of nine squares. Formally, the composition is reminiscent of Piet Mondrian's last completed work, *Broadway-Boogie-Woogie* (1942-43), created as a tribute to the jerky rhythms of New York City and the syncopated melodies of swing. In contrast to Mondrian, however, the Swiss artist broadens the palette of primary colours with mixed tones (green, orange) and breaks the grid's orthogonal rigidity by using small squares that seem to dance around the eight blocks forming the work's structural framework. While the irregular movements convey a sense of mischievous spontaneity, the coloured units are organised according to a systematic logic of permutation, rotation, and inversion. The result is a genuine visual improvisation around the motif of the square and the four colours, fluctuating between symmetry and asymmetry, between mathematical rigour and playful invention, between rational order and poetic airiness. **AS**

Bibliography

Coray Loewensberg, Henriette (dir.), *Verena Loewensberg. Druckgraphik / Prints*, cat. (Zurich, Graphische Sammlung der ETH, 22 April – 12 June 2009), Zurich, Les Presses du réel, 2009.

Coray Loewensberg, Henriette (dir.), *Verena Loewensberg. 1912-1986. Werkmonografie und Katalog der Gemälde*, Zurich, SIK-ISEA and Scheidegger & Spiess, 2012.

Untitled

1976

Silkscreen on paper, 20 × 20 cm
Inv. 2021.287
Donation Guillaume Wunsch — Monique Van Kerckhove:
Système — Hasard — Programme
© Henriette Coray Loewensberg 2023. Photo Musée L /
J.-P. Bougnet

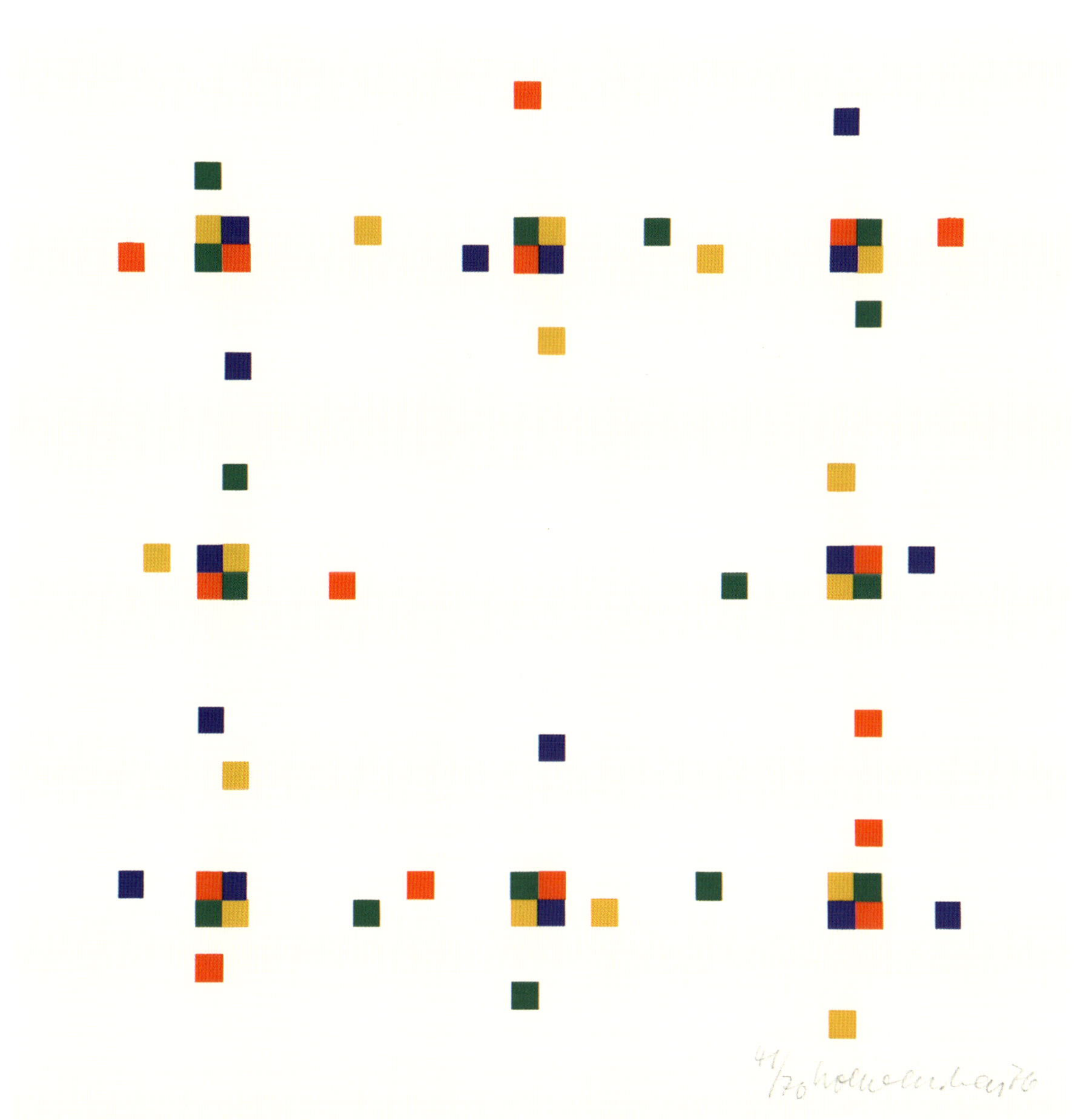

Hungarian artist Vera Molnár was born in Budapest in 1924. After finishing her studies in painting, then in art history and aesthetics, Molnár moved to Paris in 1947, where she developed an interest in abstract art, especially the work of Bauhaus artists and Constructivists. During her first few years of research, the artist conceived a system, which she called the *Machine Imaginaire*, to produce abstract pieces. The purpose of this system was to create images that were – at least in part – outside her control, thereby simulating mechanical production. But Molnár had to wait until 1968 before accessing a real computer. At the time, screenless computers still took up an entire room and worked with the infamous punched cards. Molnár then began creating geometric shapes into which she entered a minimum percentage of error (1 to 5%), in complete abstraction of the result. She honed her working method with the advent of the screen, which allowed direct visualisation of changes in the code, and, working together with her husband, she invented a specific programme called *Molnart*. She was focused on using a tool that would allow her to distance herself from her visual and cultural preconceptions.

While the artist remains fascinated by the mechanical dimension, her work retains a close connection with manual labour, allowing her to materialise what the computer has produced. The result is a fusion between painting – reflected in the execution and quotation from artists such as Monet and Cézanne – and the machine. It is worth noting that the machine is not there to serve the performance, as one might imagine when using technological tools, but, conversely, to serve the flaw. In this way, Molnár uses the machine to induce error.

This piece, *100 carrés jaunes (Computer Icône 3)*, is a monochrome of two shades of Senegal yellow obtained via this computer process. Looking at the canvas, we might ponder the very constitution of the grid: is it a structure into which the squares fit or do the squares define it? While at first glance spectators may not realise that the lines do not follow perfectly orthogonal trajectories, on closer inspection, a pattern of movement between the different squares emerges. These slight shifts produce a vibratory effect that may well reflect an analytical way of

Vera Molnár

*100 carrés jaunes
(Computer Icône 3), 1977*

transposing the brushstrokes of Impressionist artists. According to the artist, she is interested in the surprise effect that stems from the percentage of uncertainty inherent in her approach. Here, the two shades of yellow further accentuate this minimal variation. The *100 carrés jaunes* illustrate the use of the grid as an optical medium to investigate. The squares actually relate to the format of the canvas itself, challenging the intrinsic qualities of the medium. The contrast between the computer and pictorial matrices is ultimately expressed through error and loss of control. **VP**

Bibliography

Vera Molnár. Une rétrospective (1942-2012), cat. (Rouen, Musée des Beaux-Arts and Saint-Pierre-de-Varengeville, centre d'Art contemporain, 15 June — 30 September 2012), Paris, Bernard Chauveau, 2012.

100 carrés jaunes
(Computer Icône 3)
1977

Acrylic on canvas, 155 x 155 x 6 cm
FRAC Normandie Caen Collection, inv. FBN 1997-08
© Sabam Belgium 2023. Photo François Fernandez

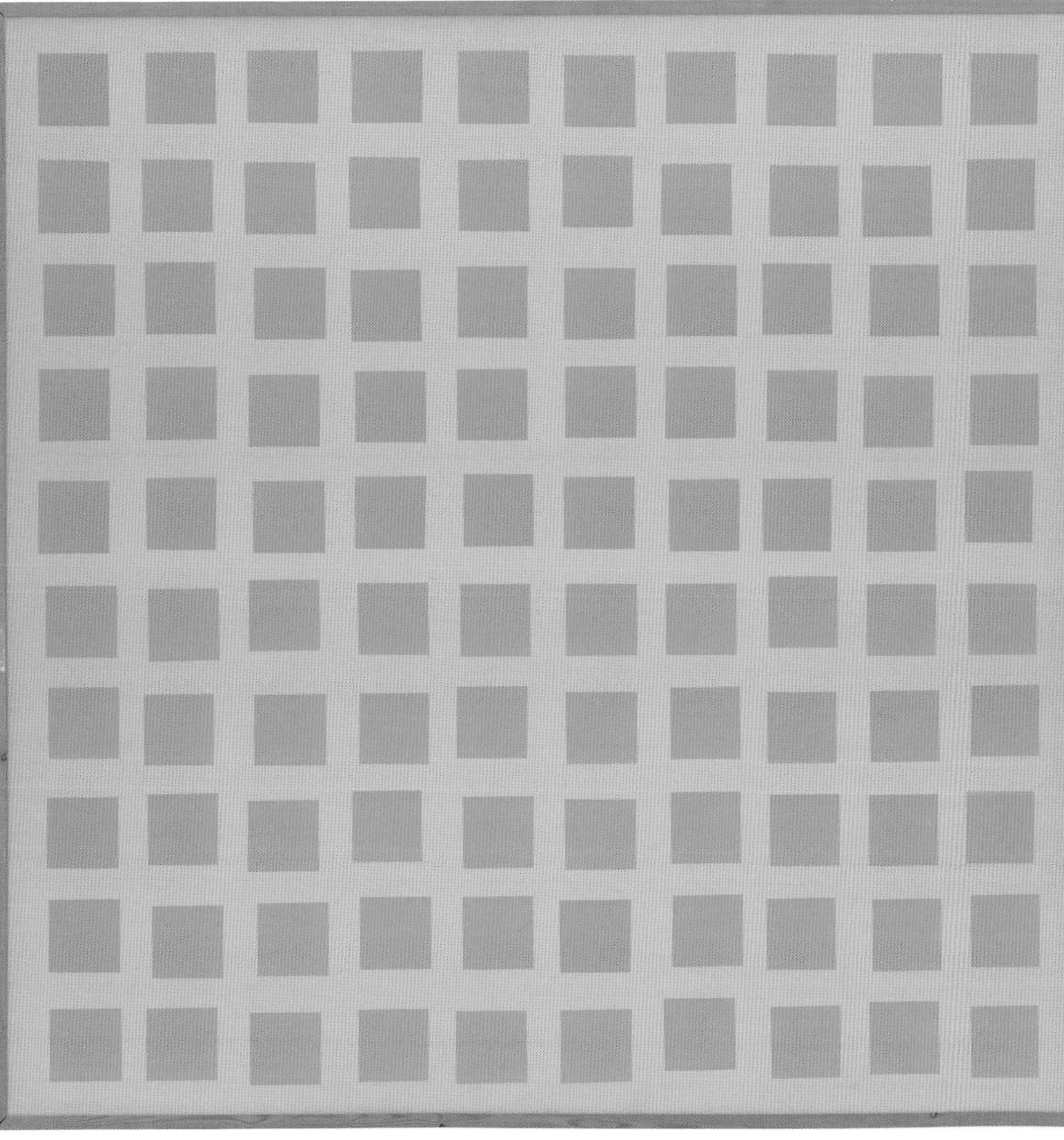

François Morellet (1926-2016) was a French artist whose work revolved around geometric abstraction from the 1950s onwards. Having previously devoted himself to figurative art, the artist adopted a geometric language devoid of any subjectivity. This change in artistic approach stemmed from the influence exerted on him by painter, engraver and sculptor Pierre Dmitrienko. Other sources of inspiration included the Concrete Art of Max Bill, which he discovered on a trip to Rio de Janeiro in 1951, and the geometric motifs of Moorish art that he admired at the Alhambra in Granada, Andalusia.

In 1961, he joined forces with Horacio Garcia Rossi, Julio Le Parc, Francisco Sobrino, Yvaral, Joël Stein and the Molnár duo and formed the Groupe de recherche d'art visuel (GRAV). The group's principles consisted of desacralizing art and the role of the artist by creating purely visual, neutral, and anonymous artworks. Furthermore, the GRAV argued that a work of art was not complete until it had been appropriated by the public. In 1968, Morellet left the GRAV when he realised that the other artists' aspirations had drifted away from his own.

Morellet felt that visual art is frivolous and does nothing to convey the artist's message, poetry, or sensibility. Instead, he wanted to offer viewers completely neutral works where the artist's intervention, creativity, and subjectivity were reduced to the bare minimum. This translated into a mathematical methodological approach where the final result of the artwork is conditioned by the system used. Having determined the system, the artist applied it rigorously, and to all intents and purposes, the work took shape on its own. Morellet's titles specifically revealed the subject matter of his pieces and represented a statement of the system he applied. Morellet did not create geometric abstract art – although his aesthetic could conceivably come close – but rather, concrete art defined by a *modus operandi* laid down in advance and applied neutrally and precisely.

As the title suggests, *2 trames de grillage -3° +3°* is a piece where Morellet has superimposed two grids on a square of white-painted wood and tilted them by three and minus three degrees respectively. The presence of the two grids creates an

François Morellet
2 trames de grillage -3° +3°,
1972

optical effect that confers a certain dynamism to the painting. The screens overlap in the centre of the picture, revealing the white background. However, the grids intersect more regularly on the outer edges, conveying an impression of density. This visual distortion is akin to that of a net supporting a mass at its centre. Furthermore, the three-dimensionality of the composition suggests a third grid formed by the shadows of the other two. These effects unsettle the viewer's vision and compel them to interact with the piece.

The systematic approach of Morellet's creative method can be clearly observed in his use of different data from a system that has been put in place; in this case, the inclination of the two grids of netting. The artist also produced the pieces *2 trames de grillage -1° +1°; 2 trames de grillage -2° +2°; 2 trames de grillage -4° +4° and 2 trames de grillage -5° +5°*. While these different compositions differ in size and colour, they are all variations of the same system.

The grid is a central theme in François Morellet's work; it is the regular arrangement of straight lines minimising the artist's subjective intervention. **ED**

Bibliography

Lemoine, Serge, *François Morellet*, Paris, Flammarion, 2011.

2 trames de grillage -3° +3°
1972

Acrylic and wire mesh on wood, 60 × 60 cm
Centre national des Arts plastiques,
on deposit at L'Espace de l'art concret, Mouans-Sartoux,
inv. FNAC 02-1291, ref. 72015
© Sabam Belgium 2023

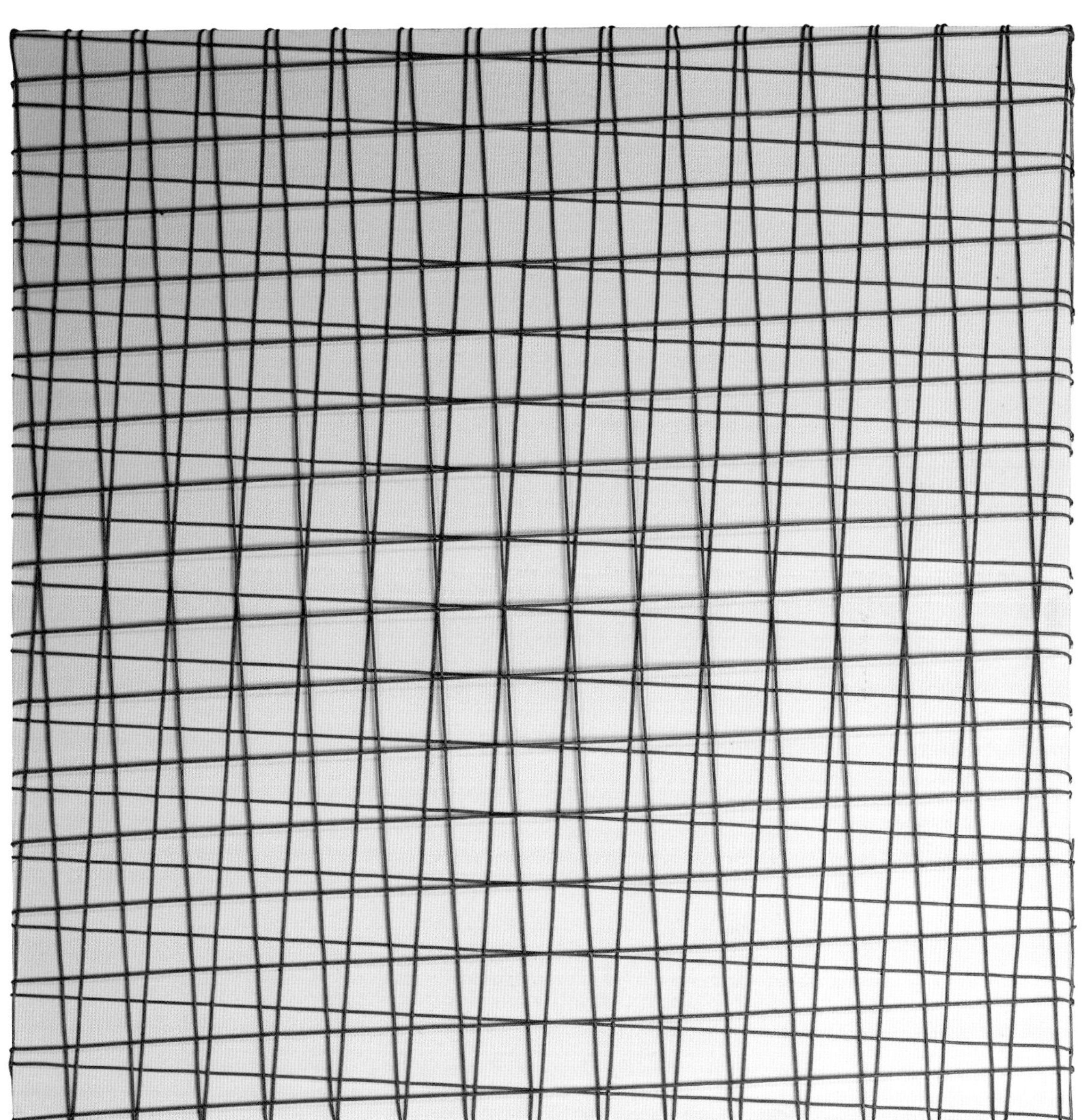

In 1966, Carl Andre said of the modular sculptures he was producing at the time that made him a leading figure in Minimalist art, "Rather than cut into the material, I now use the material as the cut in space." Andre was born in Quincy, Massachusetts, in 1935, and studied at Phillips Academy in Andover from 1951 to 1953. In 1954, he travelled to Europe before settling in New York in 1957. He befriended the painter Frank Stella, whose *Black Paintings* – minimalist compositions based on the repetition of black rays – had a major influence on his work through their formal simplicity and anti-symbolism. As Andre wrote of his friend's art: "Art excludes the unnecessary. Frank Stella has found it necessary to paint stripes. There is nothing else in his painting." The same literalism can be observed in the wooden sculptures of the late 1950s, which are made of simple beams or geometric structures based on interlocking wooden modules. These minimalist works, inspired by Constantin Brancusi, particularly the *Endless Column*, eliminate the plinth altogether and embrace the idea of sculpture as a repetition of simple elements, stretching out potentially infinitely in space. At the same time, Andre was writing poems employing language as a group of material units which, like the sculptural works, are organised according to the principles of interchangeability and permutability.

Since the mid-60s, Andre used industrially produced materials (bricks, steel, aluminium, copper, tin, and magnesium) and began assembling his modular artworks from identical prefabricated elements, which he would arrange according to the location in which they were to be presented. In 1967, he made his first *Squares*, metal plates laid flat on the floor to form a square. Designed so that people could walk on them, these plates marked a radical departure from the traditional principles of sculpture. Andre creates horizontal sculptures – rather than autonomous objects characterised by their verticality – which he defines as places or even as a road that "doesn't reveal itself at any particular point or from any particular point", but which must be physically perceived. Combining two metals of different colour, some of his pieces mimic the grid pattern of a chessboard, emphasising the playful structure of the pieces, which is based on the positional relationships between the different elements.

South Deck (1993) is made of ten metal plates, nine of which form a square, while the last is superimposed on the plate in the south-facing corner. Whereas the earlier plates were primarily based on the interaction between material, place, and the physical experience of space, *South Deck* also boasts geographical and architectural dimensions. The tenth plate introduces a certain thickness while at the same time situating the piece in relation to the four points of the compass. The word 'deck' — which simultaneously means terrace, bridge, level, and pack of cards — also evokes very specific spatial realities, such as navigation, landscaped outdoor spaces, and stacking (of cards or levels). The experience of *South Deck* is less dependent on a purely physical encounter with the work than on a mental appropriation of it, through the associations provoked by the polysemy of the title. **AS**

Bibliography

Carl Andre. La sculpture comme lieu, cat. (Musée d'Art moderne de la Ville de Paris, 18 October 2016 — 12 February 2017), Paris, Paris Musées, 2016.

RIDER, Alistair, *Carl Andre. Things In Their Elements*, London, Phaidon, 2011.

South Deck

1993

Installation made up of 10 adjoining laminated steel plates,
150 × 150 × 0.8 cm
Centre national des Arts plastiques, on deposit at L'Espace de l'art concret,
Mouans-Sartoux, inv. FNAC 02-1108
© Sabam Belgium 2023 / CNAP. Photo L'Espace de l'art concret, Mouans-Sartoux

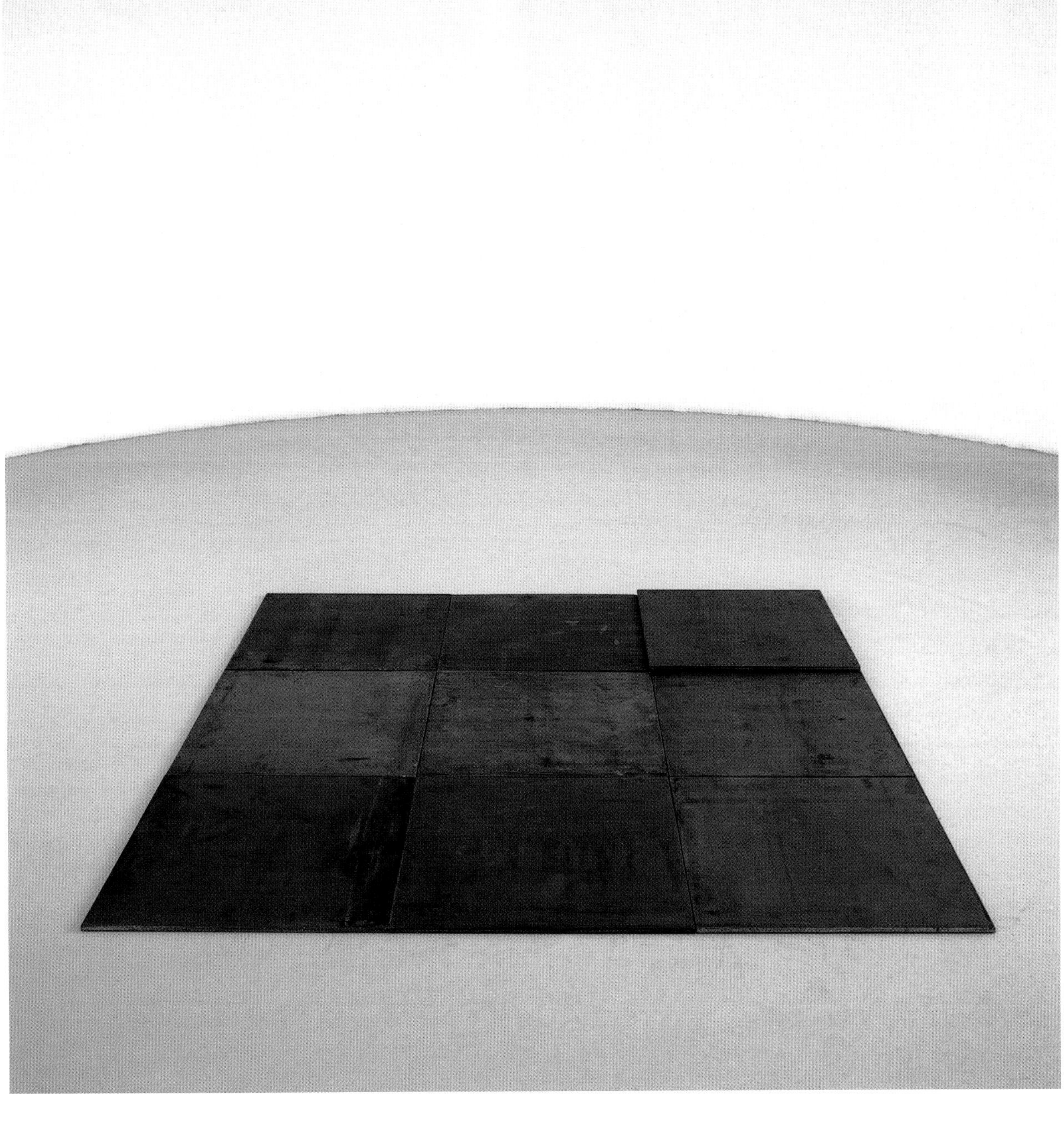

Sol LeWitt was born in Hartford (Connecticut) in 1928 and died in New York in 2007. He is considered as one of the major figures of Minimal Art and Conceptual Art. In 1953, after his studies at Syracuse University, LeWitt discovered Eadweard Muybridge's chronophotographic studies, which rekindled his interest in movement and the concept of series. In the mid-1950s, he started working as a graphic designer in the studio of renowned architect I. M. Pei, an experience that stirred his interest in geometric and architectural challenges. In the late 1950s, under the influence of Josef Albers, Jasper Johns, and Frank Stella, his style shifted from gestural painting to a more rigorous abstraction focused on themes related to surface texture and the repetition of geometric shapes. In the early 1960s, he started producing his minimalist rectangular objects, which climaxed in 1964 with the first open structures painted black to emphasise their linear framework. He quickly switched to white, a less dramatic colour more easily adapted to the exhibition space. In 1966, his *Serial Project #1 (ABCD)* signalled a turning point in the artist's work. Based on an orthogonal grid, this was the artist's first conceptual piece. Indeed, Sol LeWitt's rational system of variations on a premeditated idea relegated the material execution of the artwork to the second position. In his 1967 short text entitled "Paragraphs of Conceptual Art" which quickly became the manifesto of the eponymous movement, LeWitt stated about the artwork: "No matter what form it may finally have it must begin with an idea".

In parallel to his modular structures, where the cube and its variations are embedded in an open grid system, in 1968 LeWitt started making *Wall Drawings*, the execution of which was often entrusted to collaborators or assistants. Made up of a network of lines, arcs, circles or grids, the *Wall Drawings* span *all-over* the surface of a wall, emphasising their hybrid status between drawings and architecture. In his photographic oeuvre of the 1970s and 1980s, LeWitt systematically explored his life and the space around him. Arranged in grids of nine photographs each, the images recreate the artist's life (*Autobiography*, 1980) or celebrate the grid itself as the decisive form of the cityscape (*Photogrids*, 1978).

1-3-5-7-9 is one of a series of open modular cubes that are based on the application of a predefined logic protocol that determines the form and the structure of the artwork. In this case, the title indicates the number of cubes that constitute the length of the sides of the five modules composing the sculpture from top to bottom, while the heights of the modules are defined by a progression from one to five, in the opposite direction. The result is an architectural structure reminiscent of some of New York's modern pyramidal buildings built in the form of a ziggurat – or step pyramid – to allow for the passage of light and air. The architectural nature of the piece is further enhanced by the network of white bars forming its framework, evoking the steel skeletons and orthogonal facades of skyscrapers. Part mathematical system, part open sculpture, part architectural structure, *1-3-5-7-9* illustrates the many potential functions of the grid in contemporary society. **AS**

Bibliography

AREFORD, David S. (dir.), *Locating Sol LeWitt*, New Haven and London, Yale University Press, 2021.

GARRELS, Gary, *Sol LeWitt. A Retrospective*, cat. (San Francisco Museum of Modern Art, 19 February – 30 May 2000), New Haven and London, Yale University Press, 2000.

1-3-5-7-9

1989
White painted wood, 183 x 110.5 x 110.5 cm
The ING Belgium Collection
© Sabam Belgium 2023. Photo Hugard & Vanoverchelde

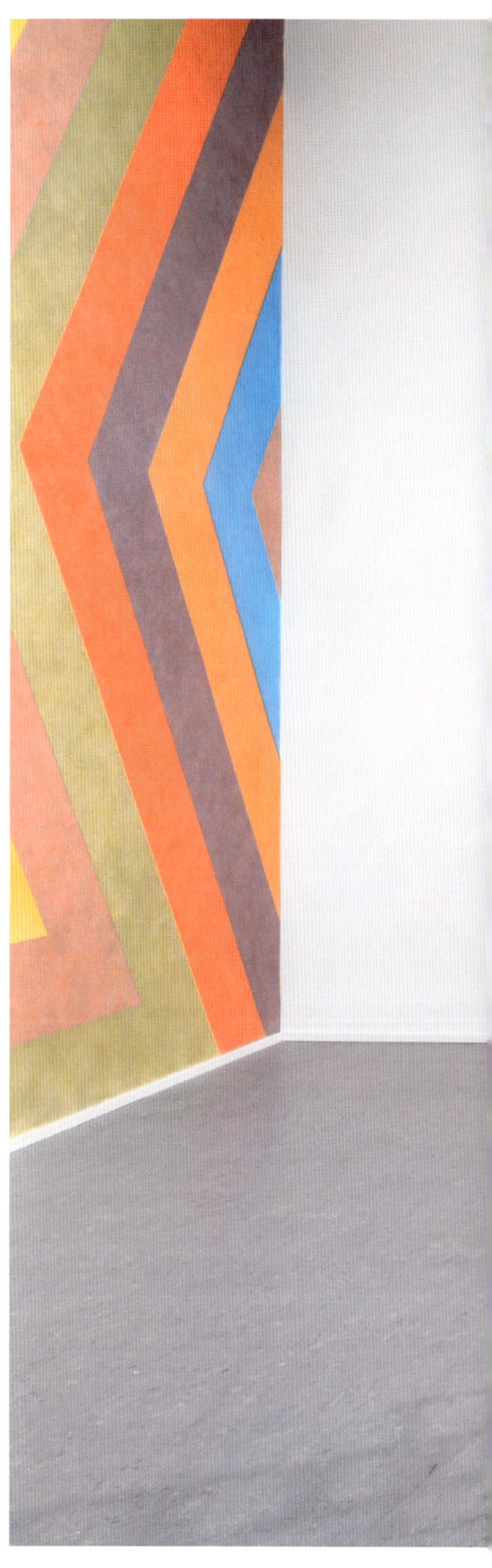

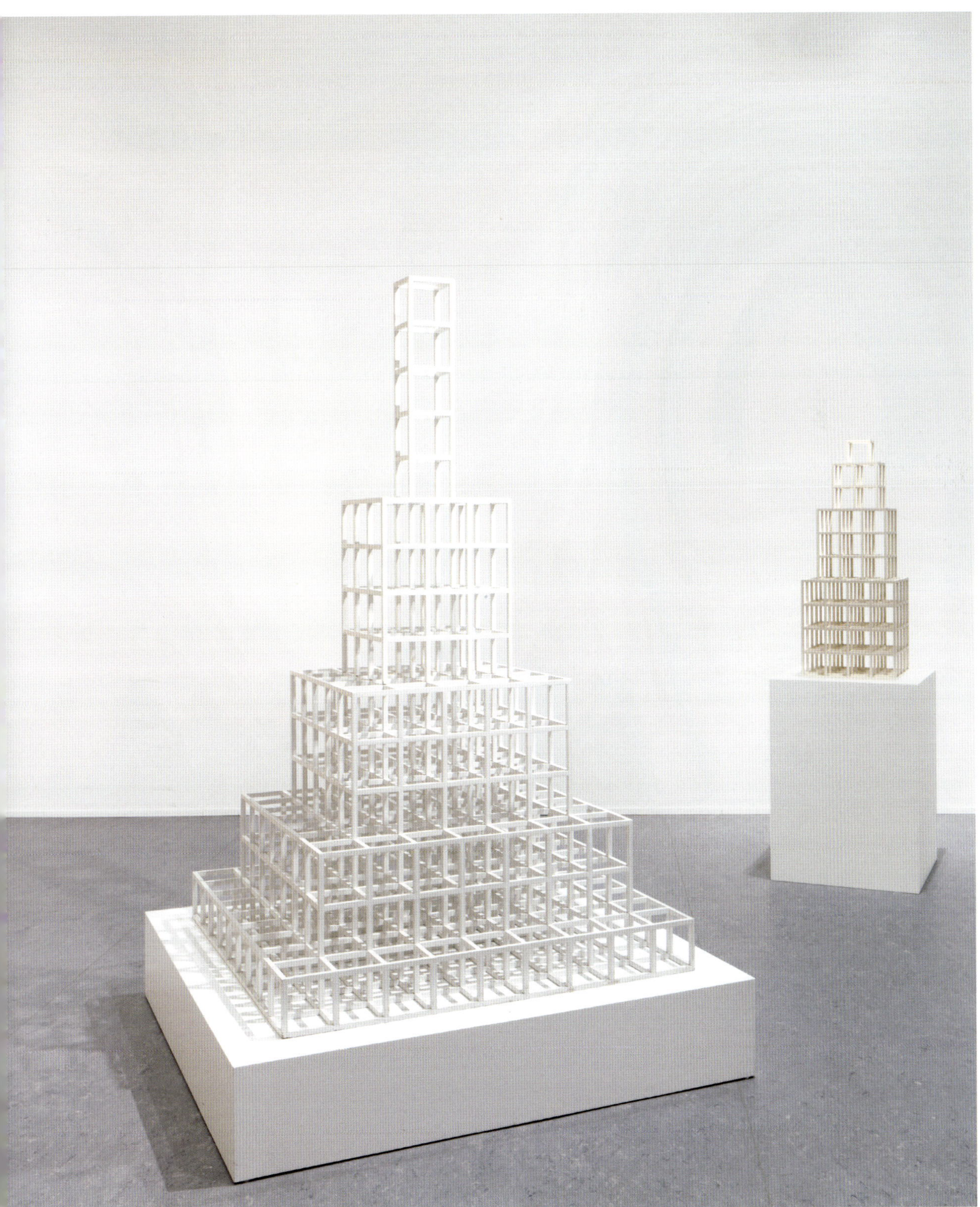

Born in Schwerte, North Rhine-Westphalia, in 1952, Rosemarie Trockel ranks among the most remarkable artists of her generation. Following her studies at the Cologne School of Art and Design from 1974 to 1978, she held her first solo exhibition in 1983 at Cologne's Monika Sprüth and Bonn's Philomene Magers galleries. Since the 1980s, she has produced a complex, protean oeuvre involving a wide variety of media, including drawing, painting, sculpture, photography, collage, video, performance, installation, and books. By combining an intuitive approach with intellectual rigour, Trockel is primarily interested in the place of women in art and society, as well as our relationship with animals, the link between private and public life, the relationship between popular culture and art, and the philosophical and religious issues associated with the tension between body and spirit, between eros and Thanatos.

In 1984, Trockel made her first knitted paintings, which earned her international acclaim. These knitted paintings use repeated motifs covering the entire surface, referencing historically loaded political symbols (the hammer and sickle, the swastika), commercial logos (the Woolmark label, the Playboy bunny), or shapes evoking abstract art (Niele Toroni's brushstrokes, Jackson Pollock's dripping). These knitted paintings provide an ironic response to a patriarchal world where men impose their laws, economically, politically, and culturally. In the historical context in which the Neo-Expressionist artists reintroduced an expressive, virile style of painting based on notions of genius and authenticity, Trockel chose a material traditionally associated with women. Trockel explored the notion of using knitwear as a subversive medium, without falling prey to the usual clichés. In response, she has developed a contradictory and fluctuating practice whereby the "masculine" sphere ("economics", "politics", "modern art") clashes with the "feminine" realm ("knitting", "craft", "decoration"). However, these wool paintings are not handmade, but computer-generated and industrially produced, a reminder not only of the production of consumer goods in a capitalist society but also of the repetitive, mechanised techniques used by Minimal and Pop artists.

Rosemarie Trockel
Untitled, 1985

Untitled refers to two distinct, even contradictory avant-garde strategies: Malevich's pure geometric abstraction and Warhol's celebration of mass culture in screen-printed paintings. Drawing on a superficially feminine technique (knitting) and motif (the rose), the tribute to these two icons of masculine modern art is turned into a parodic pastiche on gendered attributions. The Pop Art pattern, which is based on the repetitive reproduction of a single motif covering the entire surface in an *all-over* fashion, is countered by the mesh of the knitted fabric, which literally and symbolically provides the grid through which the stereotypes of art and society are reassessed. While the rose evokes the sentimental and sensual realm of tenderness and love, its serial reproduction also conjures up a sector of the luxury industry: perfumery. A rose is a rose is a rose… until it becomes a *pattern*, or a grid, which robs the individual image of its meaning, destroys its iconic value and defeats the commonplaces associated with it. **AS**

Bibliography

Guinness, Katherine, *Schizogenesis: The Art of Rosemarie Trockel*, Minneapolis, University of Minnesota Press, 2019.

Stich, Sidra (dir.), *Rosemarie Trockel*, cat. (Boston, Institute of Contemporary Art, 3 April – 12 May 1991 and Berkeley, University Art Museum, 12 June – 8 September 1991), Munich, Prestel, 1991.

Untitled

1985

Textiles (knitted wool on canvas, in two sections),
50.2 × 100.4 cm
Vanmoerkerke Collection, Ostend
© Sabam Belgium 2023

Sherrie Levine is renowned for her critical and thought-provoking exploration of notions of originality and authenticity. Born in 1947 in Hazleton, Pennsylvania, she obtained an MFA from the University of Wisconsin at Madison in 1973 and moved to New York two years later. Between 1976 and 1977, she produced *Sons and Lovers*, a series of some thirty drawings based on five portraits of former US presidents Washington, Lincoln and Kennedy, all taken from pennies, quarters, and half dollars. By establishing a link between the relationship between copy and original and the notion of the economic value of art, Levine laid the foundations for her future projects. In 1977, she took part in Pictures, the founding exhibition of appropriation art organised by the art critic Douglas Crimp at New York's Artists Space. Referring to the words of literary critic Roland Barthes, who argued that a text is nothing but a web of quotations and references, Levine proclaimed the advent of the artist as plagiarist. Paraphrasing Barthes, she writes "We know that a picture is but a space in which a variety of images, none of them original, blend and clash."

In the early 1980s, she began to re-photograph works of famous modern photographers, including Walker Evans, Elliot Porter and Edward Weston. By showcasing these photographic icons under her own name, Levine not only raised questions about the authenticity of the artwork and authorship but about her own status as a woman in a male-dominated environment. In 1983, she produced her first recreations, meticulously reproducing the works of Cézanne, Malevich, Mondrian, and other great figures of modern art in watercolour and drawing.

In the mid-1980s, Levine began producing paintings that did not imitate existing works but instead explored some of the fundamental motifs and themes of modern art. In 1986, she introduced the chessboard as the main form of her *Check Paintings*, a series of works that have evolved over the years, in a wide variety of colours (from primary tones to pastel hues), media (tempera, casein, wax), and supports (mahogany, cherry, oak, lead). For example, *Checks 1 to 3* is made up of three chessboards, the first of which has yellow squares, the second dark grey squares, and the third a mixture of the two colours. The

Sherrie Levine
Checks 1-3, 1998

orthogonal grid form and the use of principles of repetition, seriality, and combinatorics evoke the mathematical character of constructivist painting, Concrete Art, and Optical Art. However, the irregular texture of the wood lends these paintings a random, almost organic character that is at odds with modernist rationalism. The title and the wood's raw characteristics suggest the function of a chessboard, which recalls the Surrealists' predilection for games and coincidence. From this angle, it is also a tribute to Marcel Duchamp, who had hung a chessboard on the wall of his studio as an object of thought, and who wanted to give up art to devote himself entirely to chess. By thwarting the modernist grid against the surrealist chessboard, Levine foils the utopias of the twentieth-century avant-gardes, whose revolutionary and iconoclastic artworks were rapidly appropriated by the art market. Let's not forget that "check" also means "cheque". **AS**

Bibliography

Sherrie Levine. After All. Werke/Works 1981-2016, cat. (Nuremberg, Neues Museum — Staatliches Museum für Kunst und Design, 28 October 2016 — 12 February 2017), Munich, Hirmer, 2016.

Singerman, Howard, *Art History, After Sherrie Levine*, Berkeley, University of California Press, 2011.

Checks 1-3

1998

Duo oil on oak, 3 × (38.1 × 30 cm)
Vanmoerkerke Collection, Ostend
© Sherrie Levine 2023

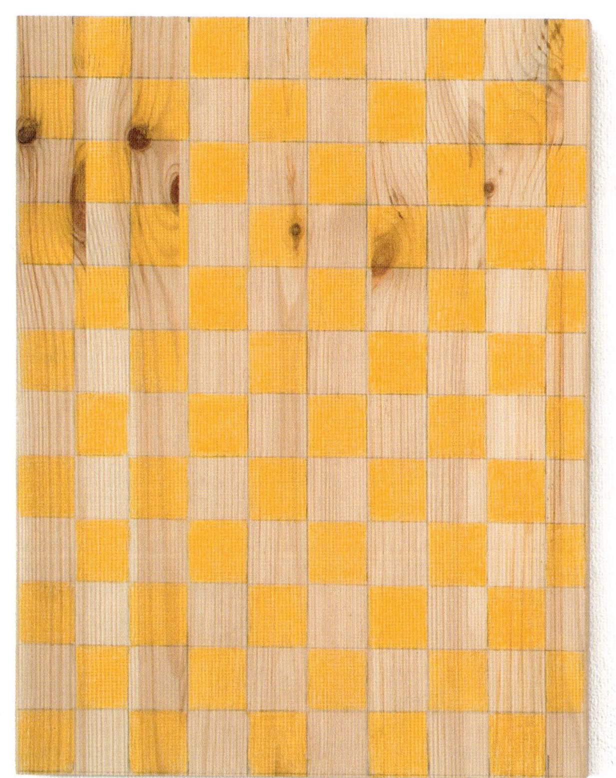
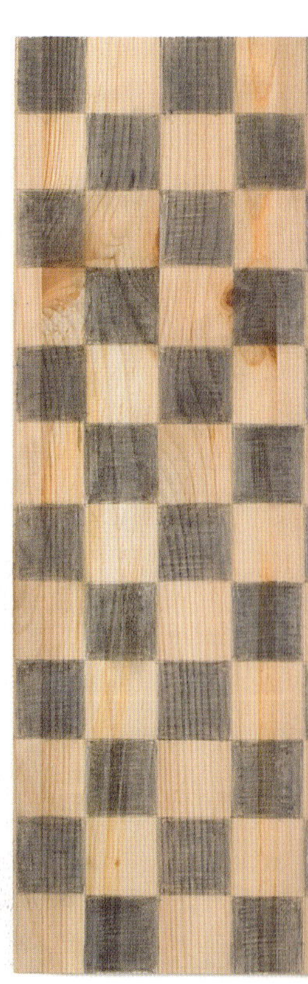

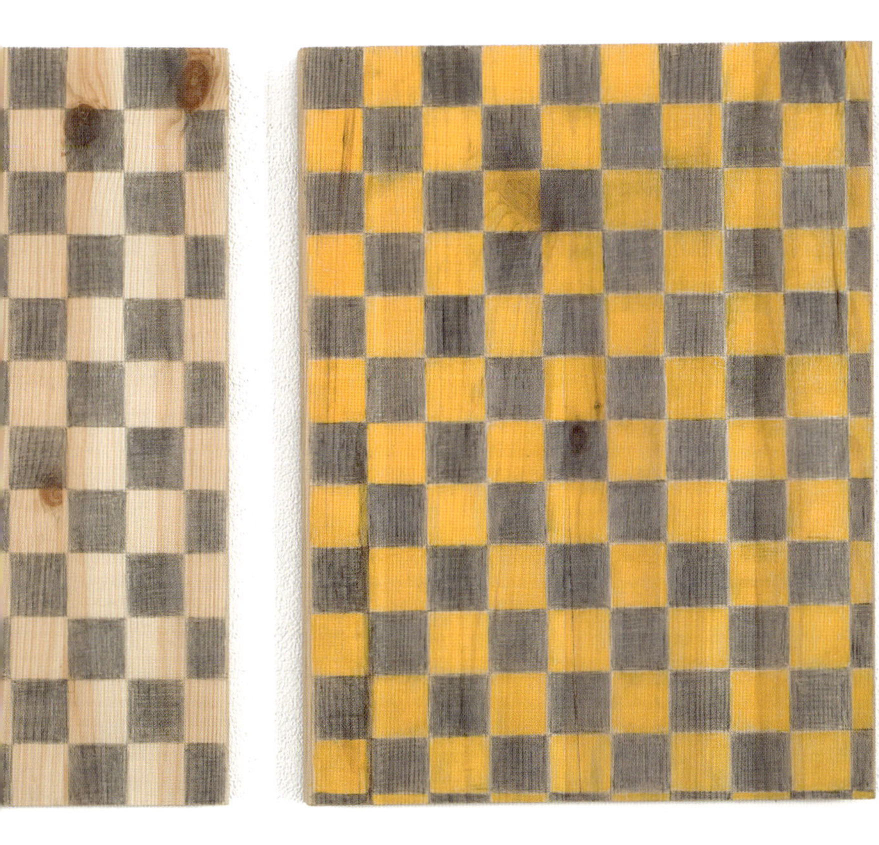

THE GRID IN ACTION

BODY, TIME AND PERFORMANCE

Throughout the 19th century, human and animal bodies became integrated into a grid system aimed at analysing, measuring, and rationalising their behaviour and movements. John Lamprey's anthropological photography used orthonormal grids to collect reliable anatomical and physiological measurements as a basis for studying, categorising and comparing human species, while Eadweard Muybridge's chronophotography was used to scientifically decompose and study the body's movement through space.

In the 1960s and 1970s, several artists associated with Conceptual Art, Land Art, Performance and Body Art turned to this representational tradition as a means of opposing traditional artworks with a documentary and processual approach. While artists such as Dan Graham, Sol LeWitt, and Pierre Cordier were inspired by Muybridge's chronophotography to analyse the body's position in a spatiotemporal system, they eschewed the rational and often discriminatory grid of nineteenth-century anthropometric photography for a subjective, anti-hierarchical narrative. Thus, the photographic grids of such conceptual artists as Dennis Oppenheim, Douglas Huebler, and Dan Graham break away from the fixed point of view and disrupt sequential coherence to introduce a multifocal perspective that also encompasses the movement of the viewer's eyes as they appropriate the work successively over time.

With its capacity to transcend the limits of the frame and disrupt a linear, unidirectional reading, the grid became the favourite presentation mode of a number of feminist artists such as Gina Pane and Esther Ferrer, who, in the photographic series resulting from their performances, created a powerful contrast between the rigid structure of the grid as a rational tool of positivist science and the associative organisation of their images, which undermine these same principles of classification and categorisation by introducing arbitrariness, heterogeneity, and subjectivity. In Analívia Cordeiro's 1970s *Computer Dances*, the grid finally appears as a choreographic matrix inside of which the dancers' movements unfold, as if coordinated by an algorithm that also dictates the camera's viewpoints as it captures the performance. Hovering between choreographic gesture and automated programme, between individual expression and orthonormal structure, the performed grid exposes the paradoxes of modern life underpinned by the contrast between subjective individualism and technological dependency. **AS**

Dennis Oppenheim (1938-2011) was an American multidisciplinary artist. Over the course of his career, he explored writing, performance, video, photography, film, and installations. As a figurehead of conceptual and body art, he frequently used his own body as a medium in his pieces. Oppenheim was particularly interested in the body's relationship with nature, space, and matter. He also works in the field of earth art, which is a variant of Land Art focusing on soil as a material. This involves leaving the imprint of the body in the soil, in the ground, as though perpetuating bodily actions in time and space.

Ground Gel (1972) is a sequence of 35mm slides complete with soundtrack. Sometimes sharp, sometimes blurred, the images show Oppenheim and his two-year-old daughter Chandra as the artist spins Chandra around clockwise at arm's length. Her body is being pulled at right angles by centrifugal force. Father and daughter's bodies were photographed from above as if they were biological cells. The succession of slides, faded in and out, creates an impression of movement.

Ground Gel captures the fading of the artist and his daughter on two different dimensions. Not only are their bodies gradually absorbed into the floor, but they also disappear into one another. In this piece, Dennis Oppenheim tackles the theme of family generations, transcending the physical limits imposed by his body. As the bodies fuse together, little Chandra is projected beyond her father in time and space and becomes an extension of him. However, the long-awaited union remains in limbo. The sequence of images is not completely fluid. Oppenheim has deliberately disrupted the order of the slides, without creating a choppy rhythm. *Ground Gel* gives the impression that each image is an extension of the next. This "stretch" – as Oppenheim calls it – echoes the subject matter of the work, which investigates generations as an attempt to move from one state of being to another.

The soundtrack that accompanies the slide show is a recording of Dennis Oppenheim's own voice. The artist almost inaudibly whispers words such as *"You're going past me soon... you're going to take me past myself... I'm going with you...*

Dennis Oppenheim
Ground Gel, 1972

Slide Dissolve Sequence for Ground Gel, 1972

I can't see you now... you've taken me past myself..." He presents his young daughter Chandra as the extension of his own existence, a means through which he is trying to project himself beyond himself since the little girl is the father's access to the future. Very poetically, Dennis Oppenheim articulates the human anxiety about the future: life is short, and man has an inherent desire to prolong his presence through images, ideas, or biological progeny.

Ground Gel was also produced as photographic documentation under the title *Slide Dissolve Sequence for Ground Gel*. While both pieces explore the same subject, the grid layout introduces a new perception. Like the slideshow, the images are not set out chronologically. Moreover, the sense of movement generated by the scrolling slides is much less perceptible here. But whereas Eadweard Muybridge's chronophotography decomposed movement to suggest it, Dennis Oppenheim disrupts the illusion of movement and reinforces the spatial effect of the grid as a repetitive, serial structure. **CAS**

Bibliography

Dryansky, Larisa, "Déplacer l'index. La projection chez Dennis Oppenheim", *Revue Intermédialités*, # 24-25, 2014, [online], https://www.erudit.org/en/journals/im/2014-n24-25-im02279/1034160ar, consulted on 2 March 2023.

Hegyi, Lóránd and Fiz, Alberto (dir.), *Dennis Oppenheim*, cat. (Saint-Etienne, Musée d'Art moderne, May-August 2011), Milan, Silvana, 2011.

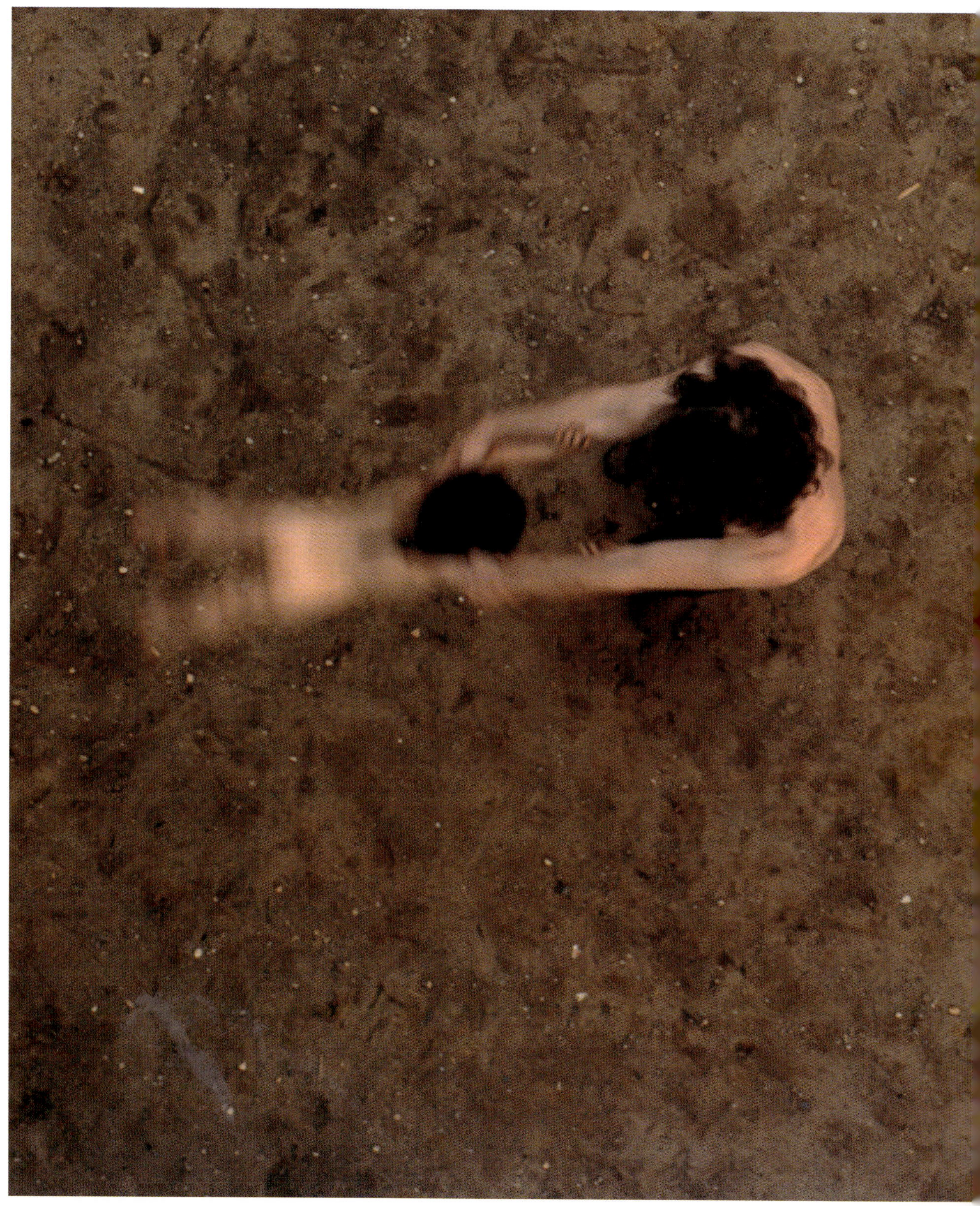

Slide Dissolve Sequence for Ground Gel
1972

Photodocumentation, colour photograph, collage, text, 97 × 185.2 cm
Collection of the Museum of Contemporary Arts of the Wallonia-Brussels Federation
at Grand-Hornu, inv. MAC-2017-018
Donation of Mrs Amy Plumb Oppenheim in 2017
© Dennis Oppenheim Estate 2023. Photo Philippe De Gobert

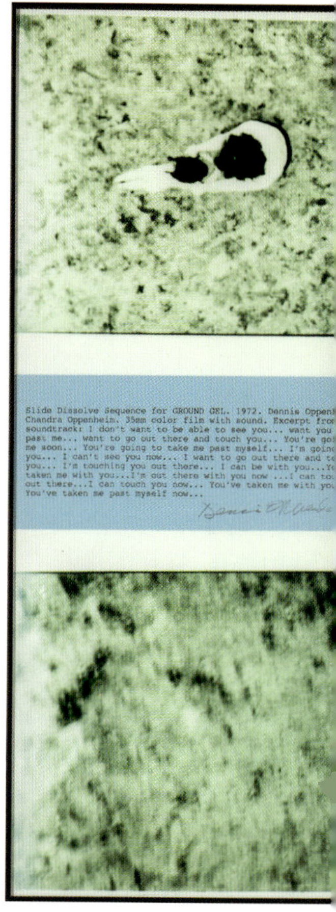

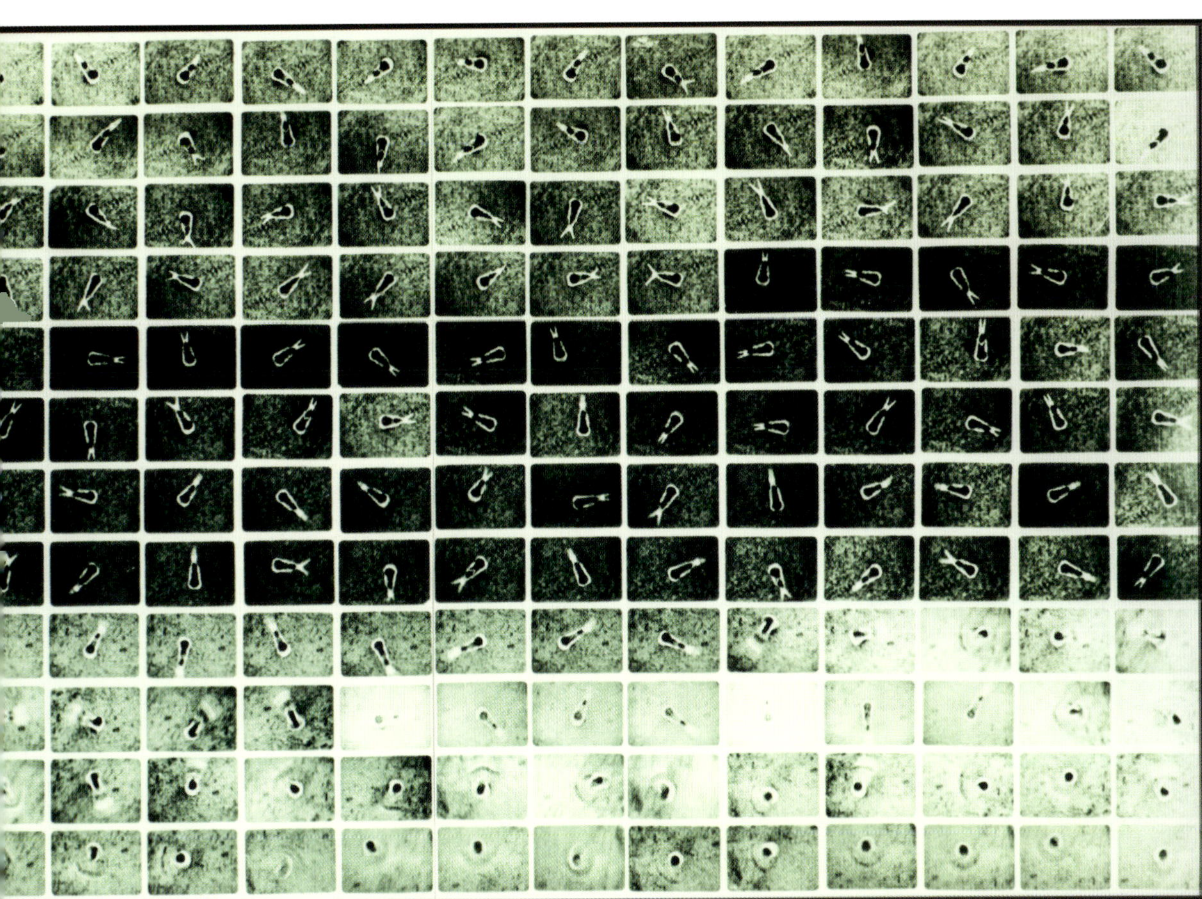

Jacques Lizène, who was born in Ougrée in 1946 and died in Liège in 2021, was a Belgian artist, photographer and filmmaker. In 1966, he advocated "art without talent" and, in 1970, he proclaimed himself "Minor master of Liège from the second half of the 20th century, artist of mediocrity and unimportance". By embracing the principles of (self-)derision and banality, Lizène challenged traditional concepts of aesthetics, such as originality, beauty, and genius. In 1967, he started producing a series of paintings on the subject of the frame to explore the specific characteristics of painting. This shift from the illusionist representation of reality to the reality of the material conditions of artistic creation were reflected in his first exhibition, organised in 1969 at Liège's Yellow gallery, entitled after a quote by Marcel Duchamp: "Il faut abolir l'idée de jugement" ("We must abolish the idea of judgement"). In 1970, on the occasion of the "Art spécifique" exhibition at Liège's Apiaw gallery, Lizène took down his canvases and piled them up to show the "other side of the picture" (the frame of the canvas) and the way in which unimportant paintings are stored in some museum storerooms (in a corner, piled up against the wall).

The cover of the exhibition leaflet features a portrait of Lizène hiding his face with his left hand. Replicated in negative and crossed out, Lizène's first photographic intervention questioned the documentary capacities of photography while simultaneously ridiculing the self-portrait as an artistic genre. In the early 1970s, Lizène's photographs, often conceived in series, presented a playful and humorous analysis of the limitations of the medium. In 1971, Lizène made a series of photographs exploring the frame as both a theme and a pictorial frontier. *Petit Maître liégeois hesitant à entrer dans le cadre de l'une ou l'autre photo* juxtaposes two shots of the artist's body – one cut at the left edge, the other at the right – in such a way that the diptych seems to simulate the action suggested in the title.

Contraindre le corps à s'inscrire dans le cadre de la photo (1971) was part of a discontinued project, which the artist described as a work with an unfinished vocation, in which he forced "all sorts of bodies, naked and clothed, including police officers', to fit into the frame of the photograph". The thirty photographs in the series are arranged in a grid in the manner of Eadweard Muybridge's chronophotographs and depict the Minor Master of Liège contorting himself until he crouches to ensure that his body does not overstep the borders of the frame, which becomes increasingly narrow as the camera lens moves closer and closer. Aside from the piece on show, there is another black-and-white photographic version of the piece, which features a nude woman in place of the artist, along with two colour films (including *Constraindre le corps à s'inscrire dans le cadre de l'image en promenade d'un côté à l'autre de l'écran*) and various more recent versions. **AS**

Bibliography

Botquin, Jean-Michel (dir.), *Jacques Lizène (Tome III)*, Crisnée, Yellow Now ; Liège, L'Usine à Stars, 2009.

Lizène, Jacques, *Petit Maître liégeois de la seconde moitié du XXᵉ siècle, artiste de la médiocrité. Tome II (Le Tome I est introuvable)*, Brussels, Atelier 340, 1990.

***Contraindre le corps à s'inscrire
dans le cadre de la photo***
1971

Black and white photographs, silver prints, 76 × 89 cm
© Sabam Belgium 2023. Courtesy Nadja Vilenne Gallery

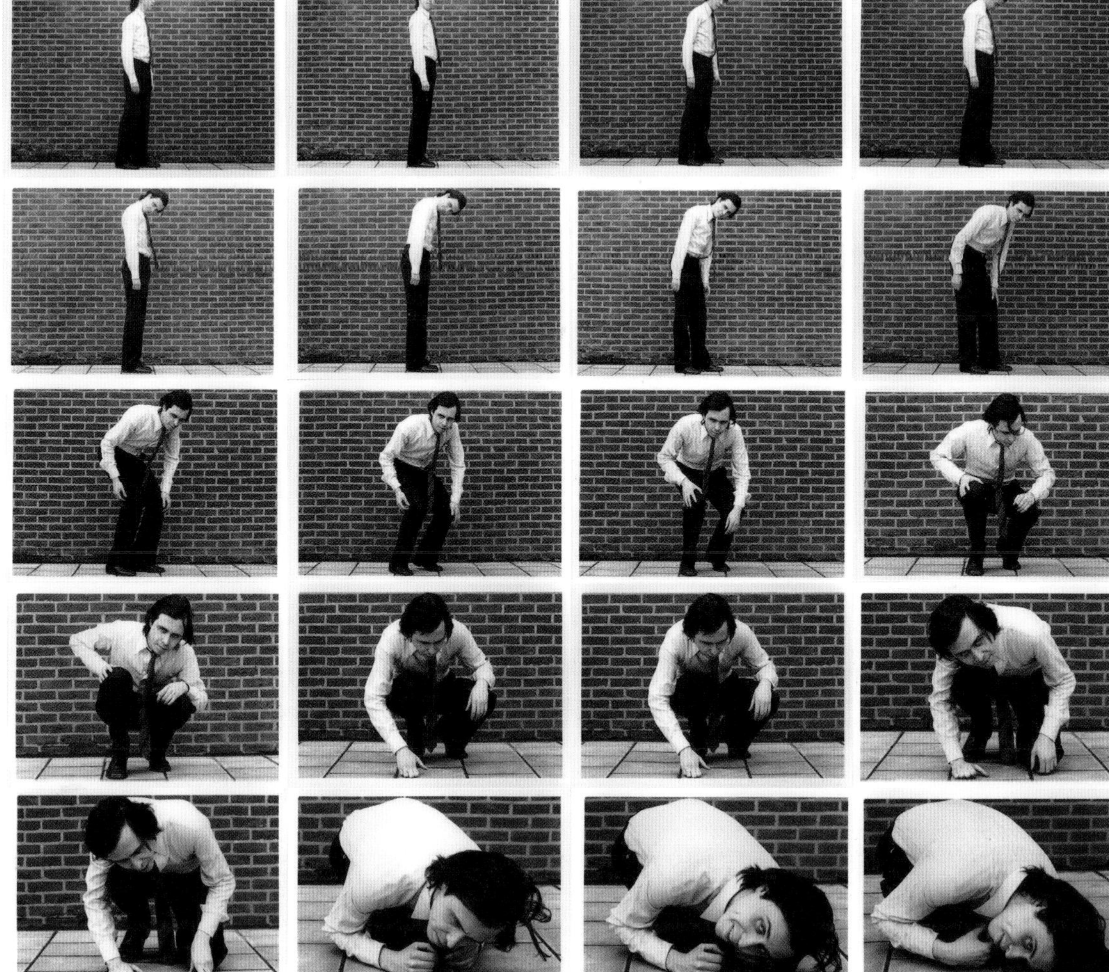

Gina Pane (1939-1990) was a French body artist with Italian and Austrian origins. Throughout her career, the artist used a variety of artistic media, including sculpture, performance, photography, and installation, although her primary medium was the body. In 1970, the artist started exploring her body and its biological properties, focusing on pain. She staged herself in various self-mutilation scenarios where she used injury to deepen her understanding of the human body, without lapsing into the extremism of the blood-soaked orgies of Viennese Actionism.

Gina Pane's *Transfert* performance took place on 19 April 1973 at Espace 640 in Saint-Jeannet, in the Alpes-Maritimes (France). In this performance, the audience was invited to join the artist, who stood in a brightly lit gallery. She stood at the back of the room with two glasses of mint water and two glasses of milk. The performance then unfolded in three stages. First, the artist vainly tried to drink a glass of mint water placed on a shelf that was much too high to reach but managed to drink some of a glass of milk, placed on a shelf at mouth level. She then tried to drink from two glasses in a row, one glass containing mint water and the other milk, both placed on the floor. Like the first attempt, this too proved unsuccessful, for no matter in which way she contorted her body, she was unable to drink from the glasses while sitting on the floor with her legs outstretched. The third and final phase of the performance succeeded: having shattered the glasses with a stone, the artist lapped up the mixture of the two liquids from the floor through the sharp shards of glass.

Here, mint – an elemental Mediterranean aromatic plant – symbolises the unfulfilled, thus unattainable desire. This frustration drives human beings to repress themselves and return to their essence, as symbolised by milk that represents life and the mother's womb. Gina Pane sought to expose anyone who saw this withdrawal into oneself as the path to utopian collective happiness.

Gina Pane's signature theme of wounds is evident in the third act of *Action Transfert*. While lapping up the liquid from the floor, the artist lacerated her tongue and bled, but relentlessly persisted in her effort. Since blood represents the very archetype of life – even more than the nourishing milk or reproductive sperm – Gina Pane was expressing the idea that man's salvation must come through redeeming pain: only through destruction and injury can we transcend a deceptive dualistic path and achieve a more viable harmony between body and spirit.

Action Transfert presents twelve individually framed photographs assembled in a three-by-four grid. Gina Pane did not consider this photomontage as a souvenir or a means of documentation, but rather, as an integral part of the performance. She explained that "the physical action was never conceived as an ephemeral work but as a mural composition produced in three stages [preparatory work, action, and photographic work]". Each photograph was carefully considered before being retouched with artificial colours in the lab. The final juxtaposition of these images is aimed to establish a dialogue between the images and give them new meaning, while also challenging the audience's perception. **CAS**

Bibliography

Pluchart, François, "L'espace mental de Gina Pane", *arTitudes*, # 5, Summer 1973, p. 16-19.

Perrier de La Bâthie, Pierre-Emmanuel, "La photogénie de l'artiste en action : six exemples de l'acte créateur photographié au xxᵉ siècle", *Les Cahiers de l'École du Louvre*, 2, 2013, p. 1-10.

Neau, Françoise, "L'action corporelle en images : notes sur le travail de Gina Pane", *Champ psychosomatique*, # 52, April 2008, p. 105-121.

Action Transfert

1973

Twelve colour photographs, 151.5 × 246 cm
Collection des Abattoirs, Musée – FRAC Occitanie Toulouse,
inv. D.1995.1.404
© Sabam Belgium 2023. Photo Grand Rond Production

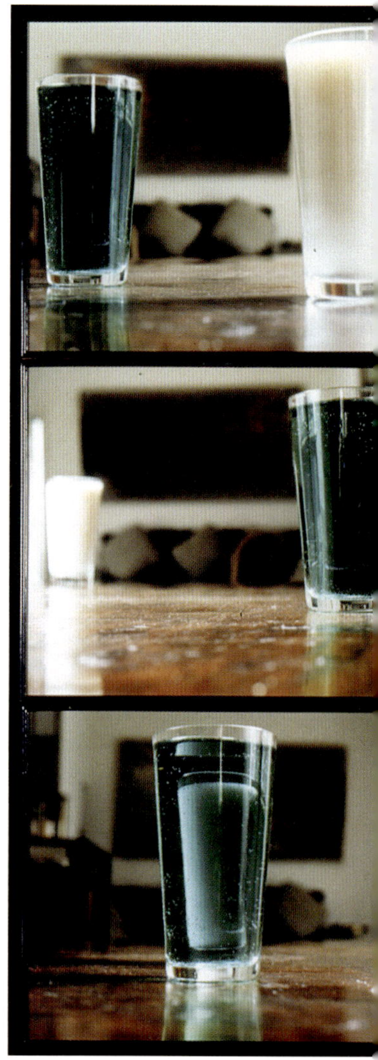

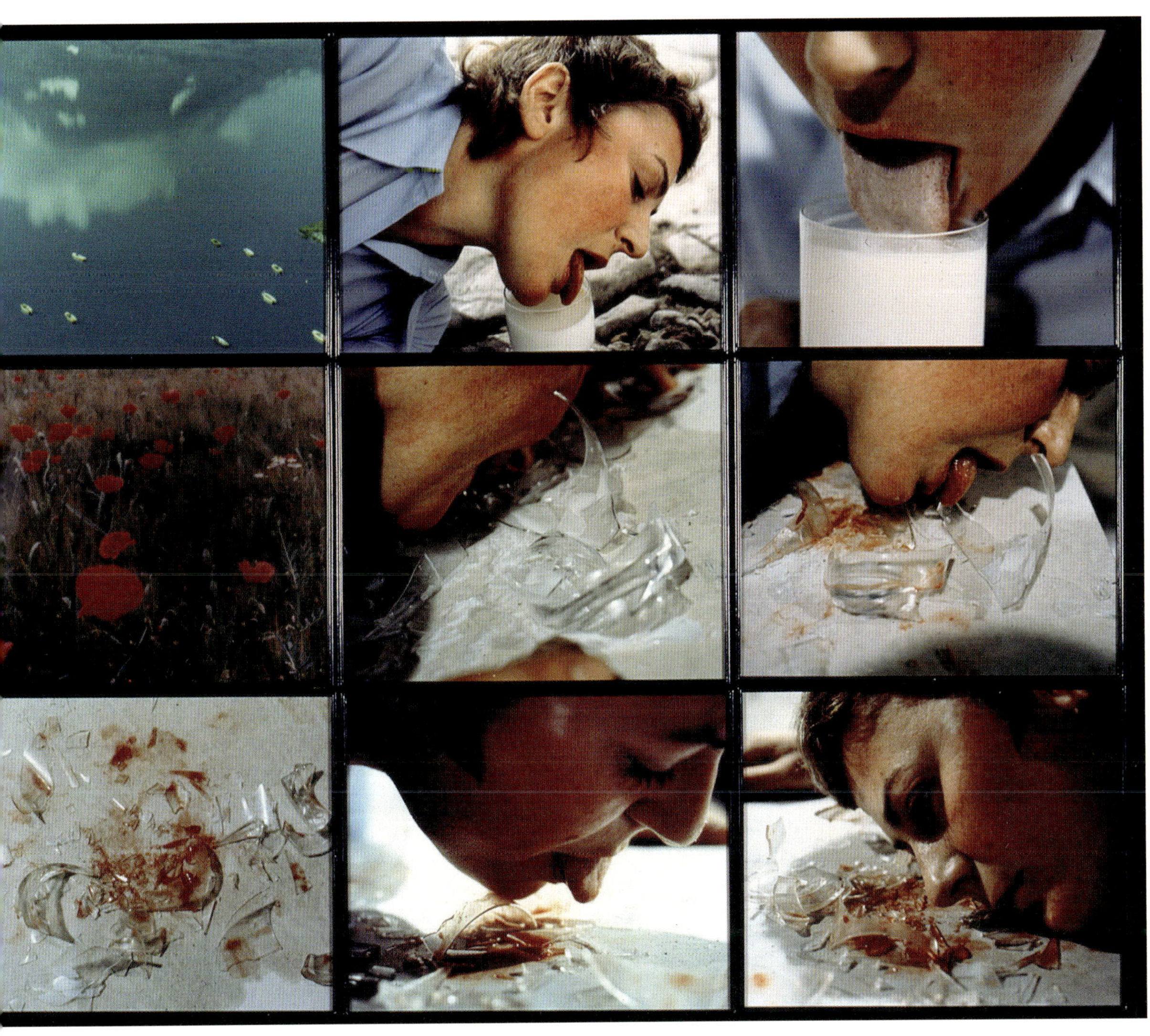

Esther Ferrer, born in San Sebastián in 1937, is a feminist visual artist and a pioneering performance figure. In 1967, she joined the ZAJ group founded by Juan Hidalgo, Ramón Barce, and Walter Marchetti, and active between 1964 and 1996. The collective, inspired by John Cage's research into chance and randomness, produced sound and musical compositions, as well as experimental poetry and conceptual practices, which were presented at concerts and happenings in the spirit of Fluxus. In 1973, Ferrer moved to Paris and started a solo career that encompassed performances, staged photographs, and installations.

In several of her works, the artist uses systems that reflect an interest in combinatorial games, exploring the various possibilities that arise from variations in the parameters of a given situation. *Permutations* is one such example. This installation consists of several panels flanking two door handles placed opposite one another in a variety of configurations: one is raised and the other one lowered, both are raised, both are lowered and so on. The handles assume an anthropomorphic form, and the whole, laid out in the form of a grid, suggests the different moments of an objectual choreography based on principles of repetition and alternation.

The simple protocols of Ferrer's performances are also subject to a wide range of variations arising from their free interpretability. *Íntimo y personal* is an action based on the subjective measurement of the body. Several choices are left to the performers and the audience: both the artist and volunteers can take part, there is no fixed duration or time limit, and the parts of the body being measured are not pre-established. Dimensions are neither objectively nor systematically determined and can be marked on a blackboard, on the floor, on the wall, or on the body with stickers in the shape of a dot, a digit, or a musical note. Rather than producing a set of logically usable quantitative data, they become elements of a score activated by the performers, who are invited to add them up, sing them, verbalise them, or perform any other gesture they choose. The action usually ends with stickers being affixed to the body, to form the words of the "intimate and personal" title.

Esther Ferrer

Permutations, 1989 / 2020

Íntimo y personal, 1977

Ferrer's non-functional measurement operation invites us to consider the body beyond the criteria of beauty embodied in physiognomic imperatives or harmonious proportions. In effect, *Íntimo y personal* is a critique of the cult of the ideal body, and particularly the projections of the male gaze onto the female body, enshrined in the long iconographic tradition of the nude and still widely conveyed through advertising and popular culture. First conceived in 1967 but produced for the first time in 1977 at the Fernando Lerín studio in Paris, the action keeps on showing, in each repetition, the persistency of such oppressive and excluding aesthetic canons. Indeed, in 1992, when the artist performed the action at the age of 55, some people present were shocked by the sight of a mature woman revealing her nudity, thus addressing the taboo of the ageing body, its representation and its social signification. **OA**

Bibliography

FERRER, Esther, *Esther Ferrer, De la acción al objeto y viceversa*, cat. (Koldo Mitxelena Kulturunea, 4 December 1997 – 4 February 1998), San Sebastian, Koruko Aizarna, 1997.

SERRANO, Ángel (coord.), *Esther Ferrer. All Variations are Valid. Including this one*, cat. (26 October 2017 – 25 February 2018), Madrid, Museo Nacional de Arte Reina Sofía, 2017.

Permutations

1989 / 2020

Installation: 9 frames, 9 pairs of door handles, text,
variable dimensions
FRAC Franche-Comté Collection, inv. 2020-1-1
© Sabam Belgium 2023. Photo Blaise Adilon

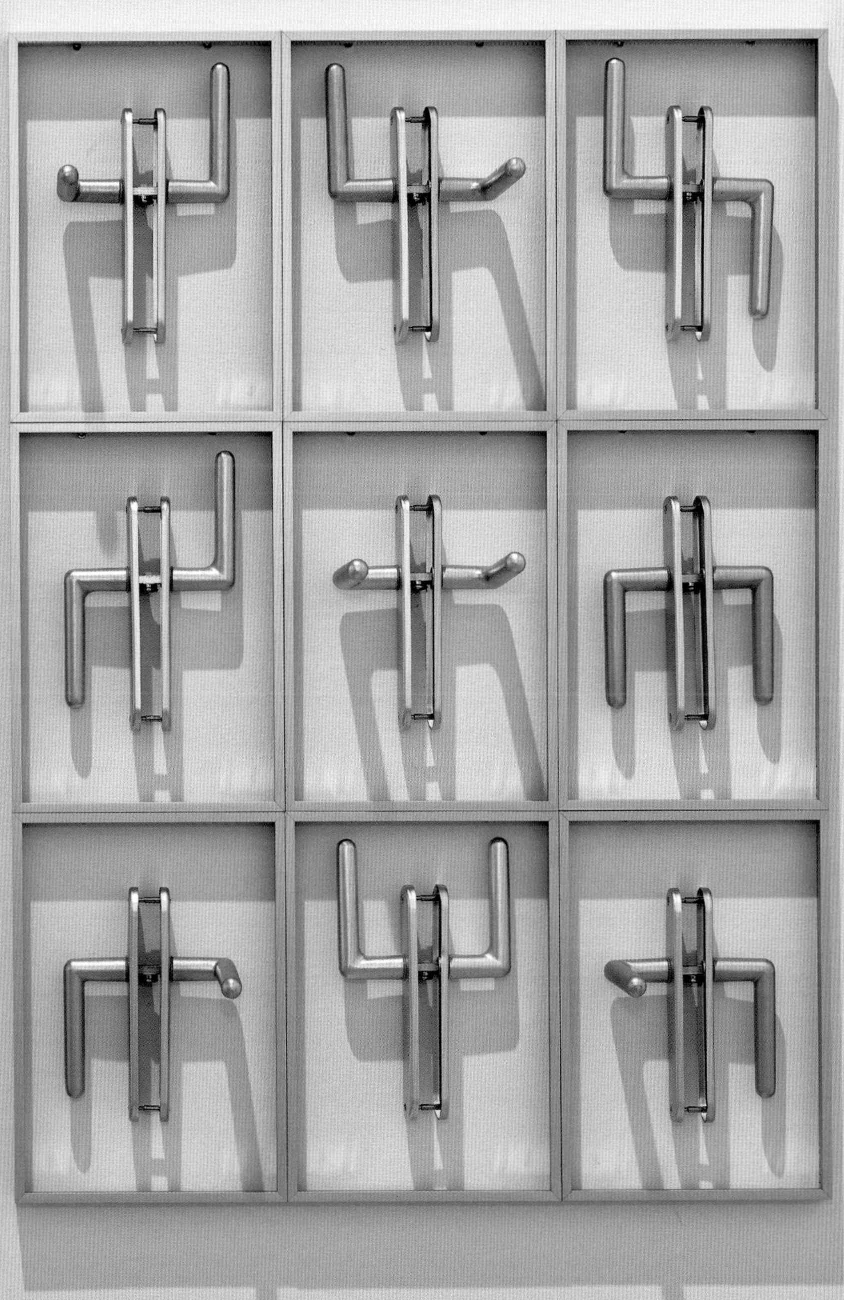

Íntimo y personal
_1977_

Letterpress and gelatine-silver print on paper, 141 × 141 cm
Collection 49 Nord 6 Est – FRAC Lorraine, Metz,
inv. 2004-04 02 (02)
© Sabam Belgium 2023. Photo Rémi Villaggi

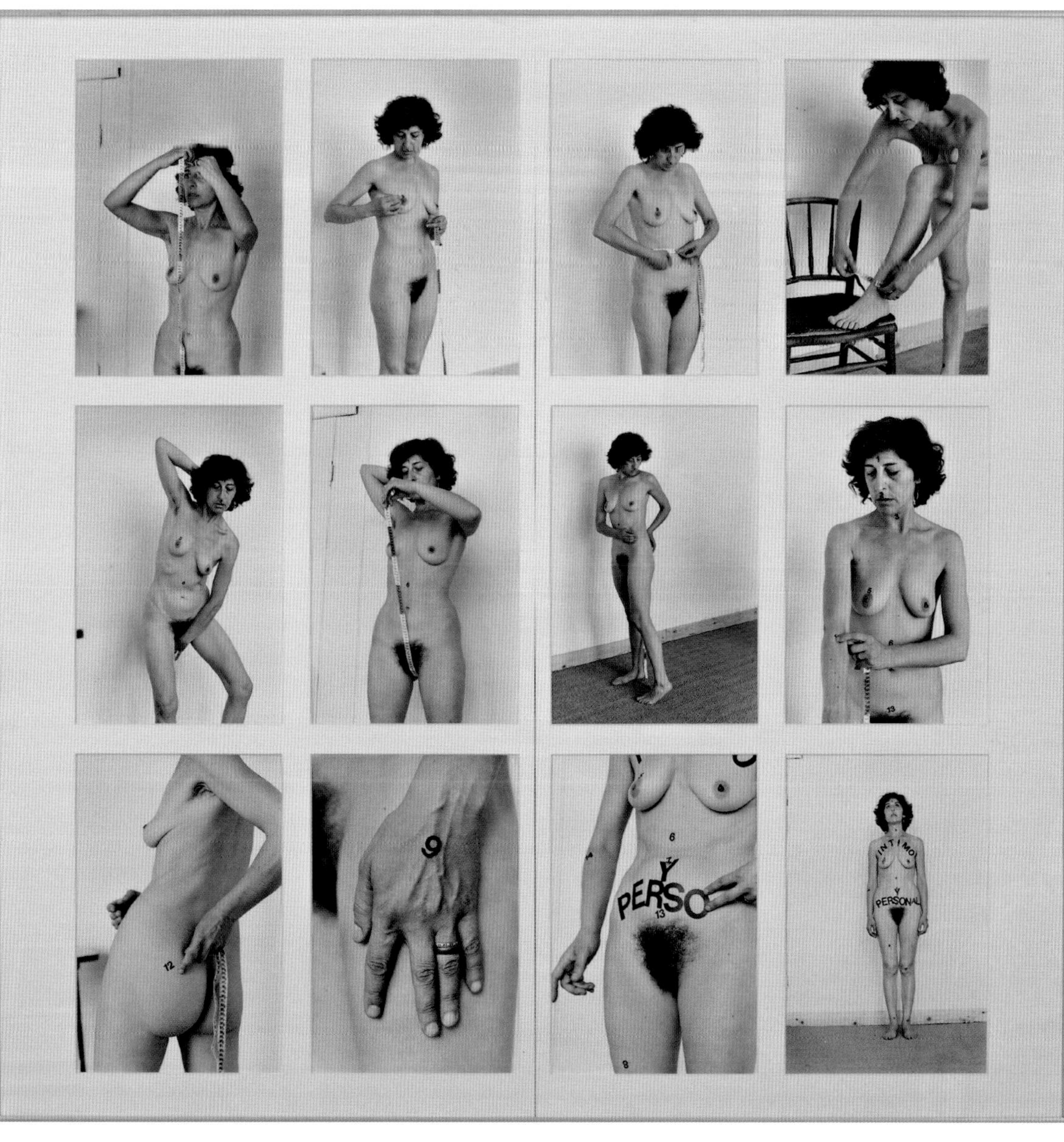
PERSO
INTIMO
PERSONAL

Born in 1953 in São Paulo, Analívia Cordeiro pioneered video art and video dance as well as computer programming applied to choreographic composition. While the use of logic systems and new technologies echoes the work of her father, Waldemar Cordeiro – one of the emblematic figures of the Ruptura group of Paulista concretists in the 1950s – the artist applies these ideas to corporality, gestuality and the study of movement. Her computer-programmed choreographic compositions resonates with the work of engineers such as Michael Noll, who started developing computer ballets in the 1960s.

However, the specificity of Cordeiro's work lies not only in the fusion of dance, abstraction and computer technology, but also in her solid training in the notation, composition and techniques of the body, particularly *Labanotation*. The artist developed her own method of machine-mediated choreographic composition. In a 1977 article entitled "Choreographer as Programmer", Cordeiro sets out this approach, whereby bodily parameters such as the dancers' positions and movements are entered in the same way as the camera's points of view, the transition between shots, and any visual effects. The algorithm then creates a score in the form of precise, interdependent instructions for the dancers, the cameras and the television broadcast.

The abstract and non-narrative video work *M3x3* is the most emblematic of Cordeiro's *computer dances*. Shot in the TV Cultura studios, nine dancers clad in black overalls are positioned in a 3 x 3 metre square grid composed of black lines drawn on the white studio floor and wall. The high contrast effect of these scenographic choices accentuates the graphic, two-dimensional nature of this saccadic dance. The homogenised silhouettes execute rectilinear postures evoking matchstick figures or automatons. They alternate machinelike poses to the rhythmic, monotonous beat of a metronome. These movements are synchronised with changes in the camera's angle of view – sometimes showing frontal shots, sometimes from above. Intended for widespread broadcast on one of Brazil's major public television channels, this robotic dance inside a wire-frame structure reflected the state of surveillance and control in force during the military dictatorship (1964-1985). In spite of the seemingly austere gestures, set design and computerised compositional process, the dancers were given a degree of freedom in the execution of their movements, and the set's grid is not strictly orthogonal. The rigid structure of a predetermined choreography is challenged by subjective factors, such as the performers' capacity to interpret instructions and concrete circumstances. In this sense, M3x3 epitomises the dichotomy between alienation and freedom, between theory and practice. **OA**

Bibliography

Cordeiro, Analívia, *Analívia Cordeiro. Human Motion – Impression/expression*, 2nd edition, São Paulo, 2018.

Pedrosa, Adriano, Bryan-Wilson, Julia and Ardui, Olivia (publishers), *Histórias da dança. Catálogo*, Vol. I and II, São Paulo, MASP, 2020.

M3x3

1973

Black and white video 4:3 (12'32"), sound
Anita Beckers Gallery, Frankfurt

Photograph of the filmed performance,
gelatine-silver print, 18 × 23.5 cm
Fundación Museo Reina Sofía, 2016
(donated by Susana Leirner and Ricardo Steinbruch)
© Analívia Cordeiro 2023

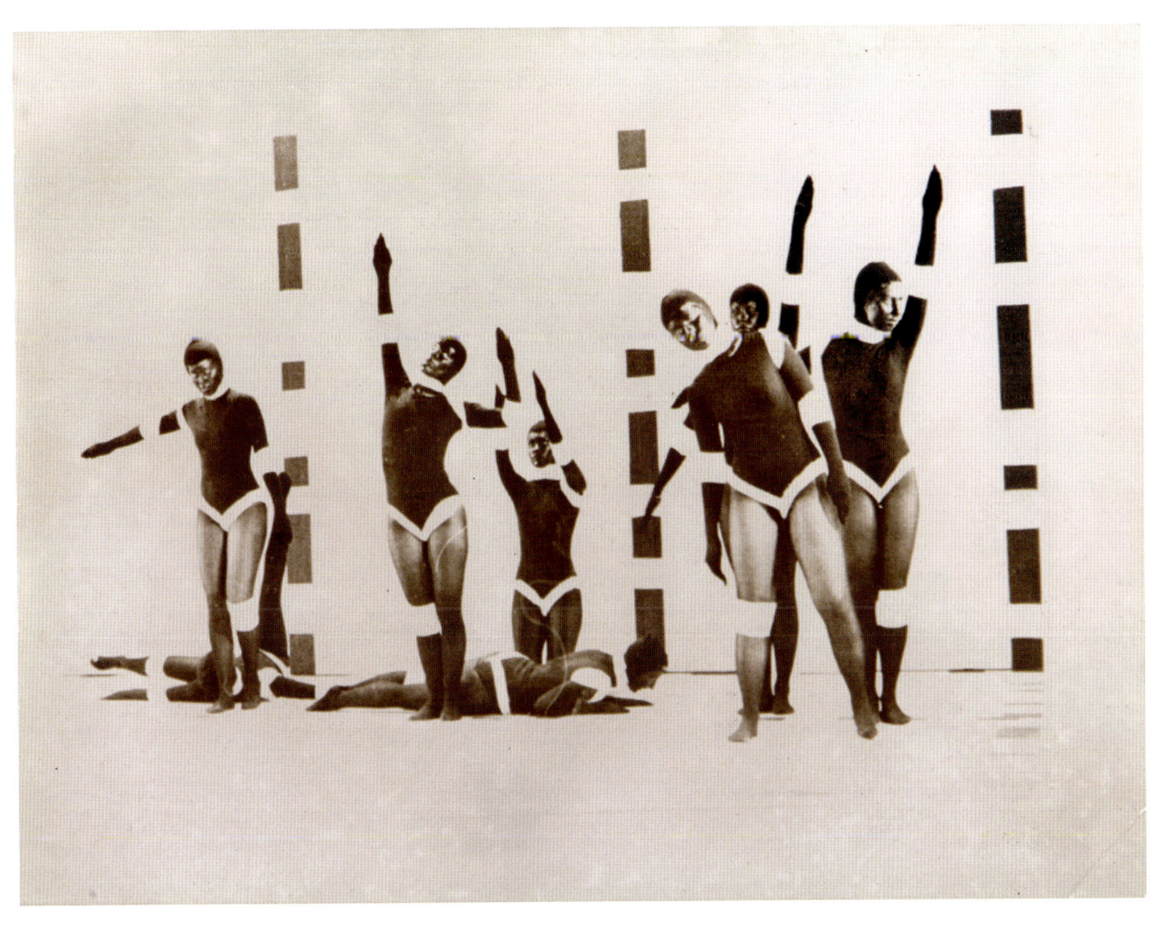

MATRIXES OF MEMORY AND IDENTITY

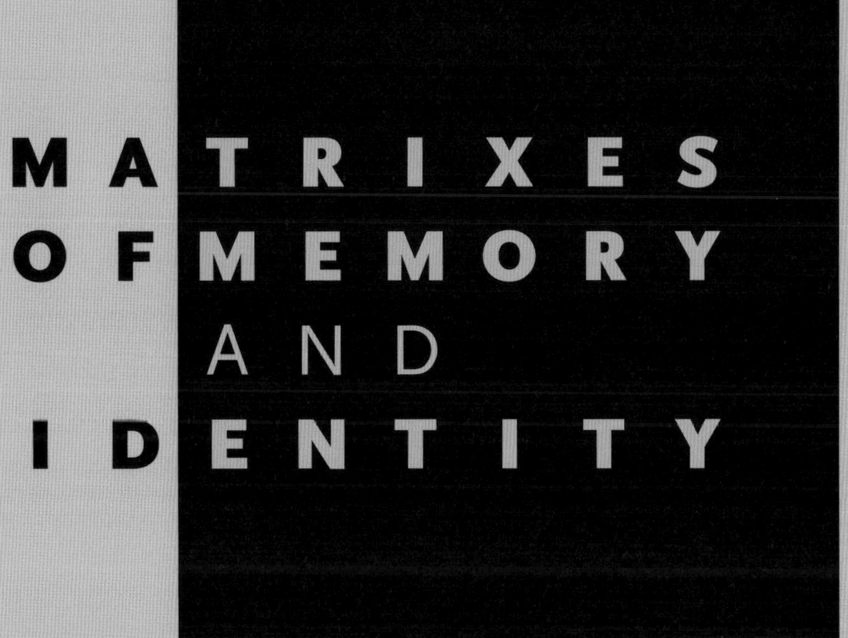

From forensic photography to facial recognition, from family albums to commemorative portraits, the uses and functions of grid compositions are legion in our visual culture. During the 19th century, the photographic grid played a considerable role in the emerging field of criminology, which aimed, on the one hand, to show that delinquency was based on physiological and anatomical characteristics (Cesare Lombroso) and, on the other, to classify delinquents in a vast system of records based on anthropometric measurements and a standardised photographic process (anthropometry).

The artists in this section are interested in these systems of identification and in the way in which identity is constructed and reconstructed through representational matrices. They challenge us to reflect on the historical, social, political, and psychological conditions that shape our image of ourselves and the Other. Since 1971, Christian Boltanski has been exploring the issues of reconstructing the past and building identity through the photographs found in family albums, "images of family rituals [...] that take us back to our own memories" (Boltanski). Presented in the form of a grid, Boltanski's photographic pieces simultaneously evoke the organisation of images in family albums and the photographic plates of the human races as one might find in an encyclopaedia. By disrupting the systematic or chronological order of these systems, the artist restores the individuality and mysterious aspect of these anonymous subjects.

The work of Anna Bella Geiger and Claudia Andujar follows a more politically charged path. In the *Marcados* series on the indigenous Yanomami people, Andujar appropriates the methods of forensic and anthropological photography. Here however, these anonymous and discriminatory classification systems are questioned by expressiveness that pays homage to the individual and decries the imminent extinction of an entire population. While Andujar's work draws mainly on the codes of documentary photography, Geiger's approach is rooted in appropriation and staging. *In Brasil nativo / Brasil alienígena* (1976-1977), the artist opposes postcards showing stereotyped scenes from the life of the indigenous Bororo people with images imitating these actions and rendering them in an urban context. This act of reappropriation exposes the artificiality of the original "clichés", while also expressing a sense of empathy that restores the dignity of marginalised and humiliated people.

In our digital age, images relating to issues of identity and memory are becoming part of the computer matrix. Thousands and thousands of images, formed from a grid structure based on pixels, are circulating on social networks, where they are brought together on social networking sites such as Flickr and Instagram in the form of potentially infinite grids. Michael Ensdorf investigates the consequences of this new digital grid economy for our memory and for the way in which we identify, categorise, and archive individuals. **AS**

Douglas Huebler (1924-1997) was an American conceptual artist. After studying painting and drawing, he turned to sculpture in 1961, eventually dedicating himself to pure conceptual work from 1968 onwards. In Huebler's view, "the world is full of objects, more or less interesting; I do not wish to add any more. I prefer, simply, to state the existence of things in terms of time and / or place". Consequently, the artist has restricted his production to pieces made up of texts and photographic images, which are often organised in a grid. To grasp his approach, we must understand his fascination with a range of notions, including time, place, and variation, which each form the basis of a series of works.

Despite its conceptual nature, Joseph Kosuth describes Huebler's approach as "impure" in that it goes beyond the strict framework of a tautological approach exclusively focused on the definition of art. This is manifest in the randomness with which Huebler chooses his shots and in the use of elusive protocols for actions which are difficult to circumscribe by words and whose scope opens up to the most varied situations. For instance, a protocol might state that the artist takes photographs "documenting the location in Central Park where an individually distinguishable bird call was heard", except that a sound cannot be photographed, and that the pictures do not actually show the bird. The viewer can therefore readily question compliance with the stated protocol and the authenticity of the images as documents. This generates an interdependence between text and image that not only reveals the limitations of the medium in terms of translating reality but also opens the possibility of relationships between the viewer and the work.

His work, *Variable Piece #11*, is based on a survey of thirty-six residents of a small American town. Here, the artist tries to answer the questions that foreign travellers might ask when driving through the town for the first time: "Who lives here? What do they do?" To conduct this investigation, he enlisted the help of the Governor Dummer Academy students. The artist donated ten dollars to the school's charities for each successful interview. Then, he randomly selected three plates. When we look at the images and read the texts of the survey, we find ourselves at a dead end: although the images seem to follow a strict protocol, the artist explains that they were chosen at random. Moreover, the surveys mention some of the portraits, but the images are not placed anywhere near the text that seems to relate to them. Thus, the grid is a key element in demonstrating the contrast between an organisation that is both analytical and random. In other words, everything seems to suggest that the portraits relate to the people in the matching house, but while the texts and houses are numbered, the portraits are not. This sort of short-circuiting is characteristic of Huebler's work, and it doesn't just serve to show us the limits of these two media, but rather to harness our imagination to a situation. As though he were sitting on a bench watching passers-by and imagining who they are, Huebler refuses to impose authority on reality, leaving each viewer free to construct their own representation of the world. **VP**

Bibliography

Douglas Huebler, "Variable", etc., cat. (11 December 1992 – 15 February 1993), Limoges, FRAC Limousin, 1992.

Lejeune, Anaël, Streitberger, Alexander and Viart, Christophe (dir.), *L'art de Douglas Huebler : « ready-mades culturels »*, Rennes, PUR, 2018.

Variable Piece #11

1971

Chromogenic photograph on photo paper, offset print,
109.5 × 104 cm and 27 × 19.5 cm
SMAK Collection, Museum of Contemporary Art, Ghent
© Sabam Belgium 2023

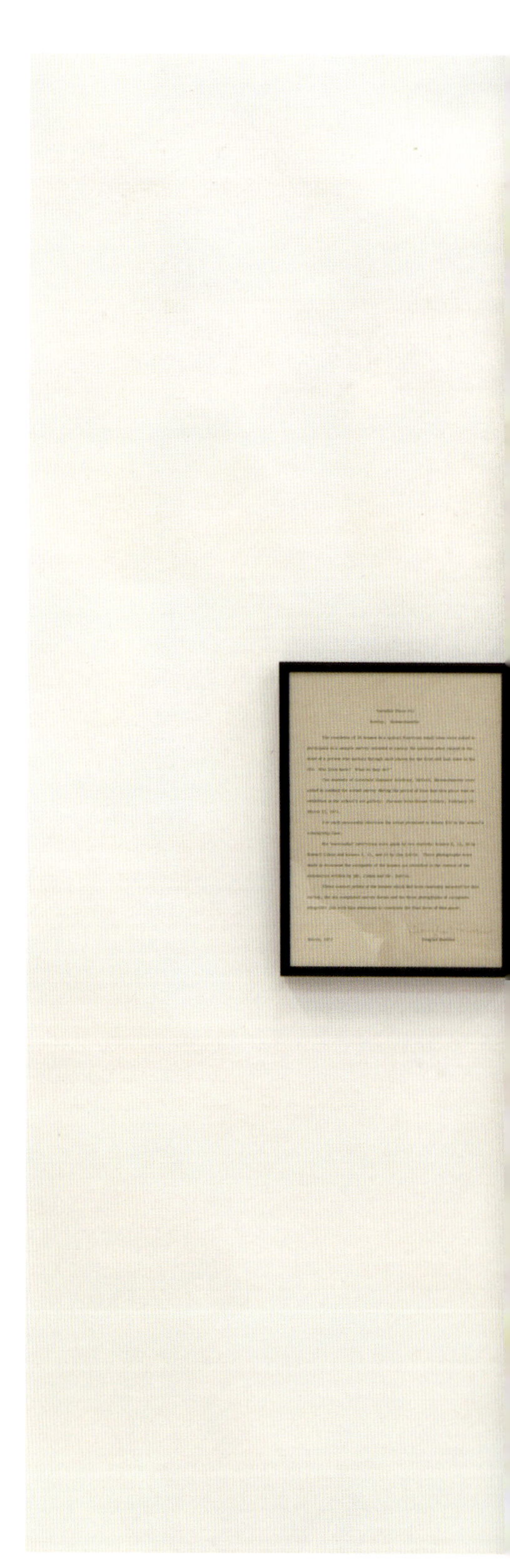

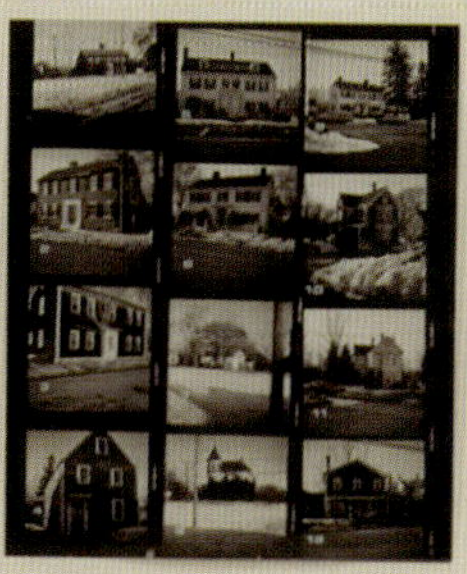

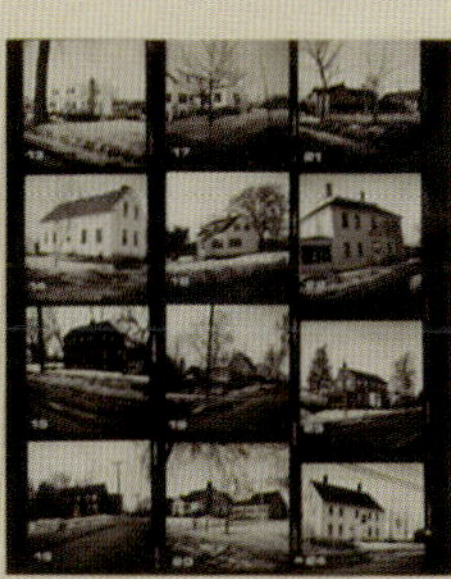

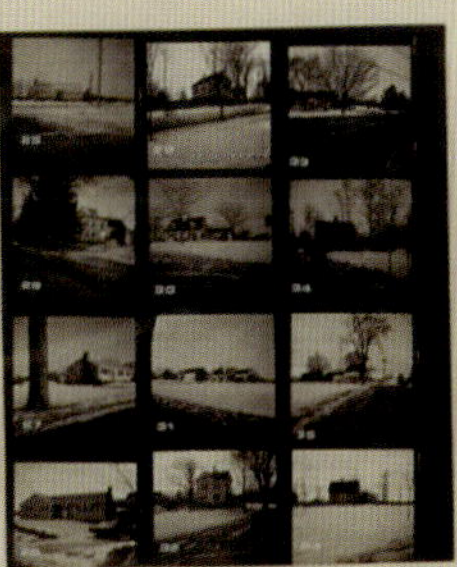

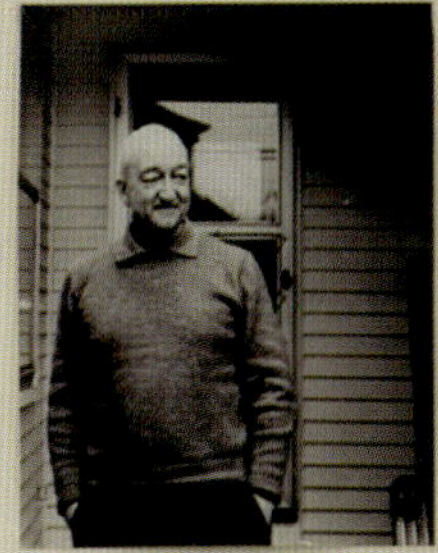

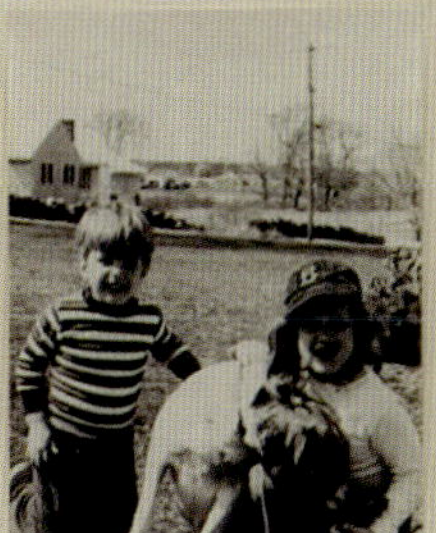

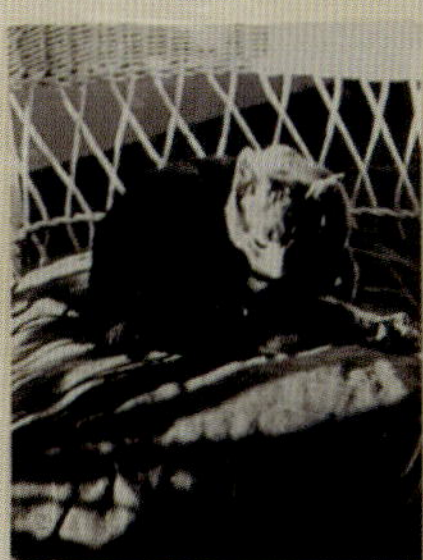

In the late 1960s, Christian Boltanski, who was born in Paris in 1944 and died in the same city in 2021, began producing a body of work that focused on the life and death of each and every one of us, emphasising everyday events. He exploited this theme by creating myths representing the universality of mankind and by the nearly obsessive archiving of human memory. In the words of Christian Boltanski, "to be an artist is to be the mirror of others."

Born during World War II to a Jewish father, the artist was scarred since childhood by the trauma of the German threat, which would shape his artistic practice throughout his career. However, the latter only really took off after the 1969 publication of his book *Recherches et présentation de tout ce qui reste de mon enfance* (Research and presentation of all that remains of my childhood). Published by gallery owner and publisher Claude Givaudan, the book featured photographs taken from people outside the family, since the Boltanskis had no photo album of their own. At the start of his career, Boltanski dedicated his life to constructing a phantasmagorical representation of childhood, far removed from his own. His sole intention was to create false memories by becoming part of the mass of normal French youth. He developed an ideal of universality that everyone could identify with.

In addition to creating mythical figures of childhood and the family, Boltanski also turned to archiving different human traces. He drew inspiration from the presentation of the collection at Paris' Musée de l'Homme to create display cases inventorying and exhibiting everyday objects as they were. By collecting these objects, Boltanski sought to counter the oblivion of death. However, this process of archiving cannot compensate for the absence that death leaves behind because the individuals themselves are not present in the artwork.

Les 62 membres du Club Mickey en 1955, les photos préférées des enfants (The 62 members of the Mickey Club in 1955, children's favourite photos) is composed of photos submitted each week by readers of the *Journal de Mickey* for the "my favourite photo" section, which Boltanski collected. The artist enlarged

Christian Boltanski
Les 62 membres du Club Mickey en 1955, les photos préférées des enfants, 1972

these photos, framed them, and assembled them into a series that represents a universal ode to childhood. Concurrently, the work also illustrates the tragedy of its disappearance, for each of the children represented has now grown up and become an adult.

This ambivalence surrounding childhood and its mourning finds an echo in Boltanski's project with pupils from the Collège des Lentillères in Dijon. In 1973, he commissioned a photographic portrait of each of the children and installed them in the school. In 1985, he used these photographs to create a photographic installation that implicitly referred to the victims of the Shoah.

For Boltanski, amateur photographs represent both material objects and a process that have enabled him to invent an art of memory as well as a form of investigation into a forgotten past. By gleaning and collecting testimonies, he sought to give a posthumous existence to people and events. Here, the grid serves as a space for encounters and connections between various individuals. The different photographs build up a single image of a universal childhood, while simultaneously allowing the children to exist independently inside the image. **ED**

Bibliography

Blistène, Bernard, *Christian Boltanski : Faire son temps*, cat., Pompidou Centre, Paris, 13 November 2019 — 16 March 2020, Paris, Centre Pompidou, 2019.

Garcia, Adela Abella, « Christian Boltanski : un artiste contemporain vu et pensé par une psychanalyste », Revue française de psychanalyse, 2008/4 (vol. 72), p. 1113-1135.

Semin, Didier, *Christian Boltanski*, London, Phaidon, 1997.

**Les 62 membres
du Club Mickey en 1955,
les photos préférées
des enfants**
1972

60 black and white photographs,
60 × (30.5 × 22.5 cm)
FRAC Grand Large — Hauts-de-France, inv. 83.75
© Sabam Belgium 2023

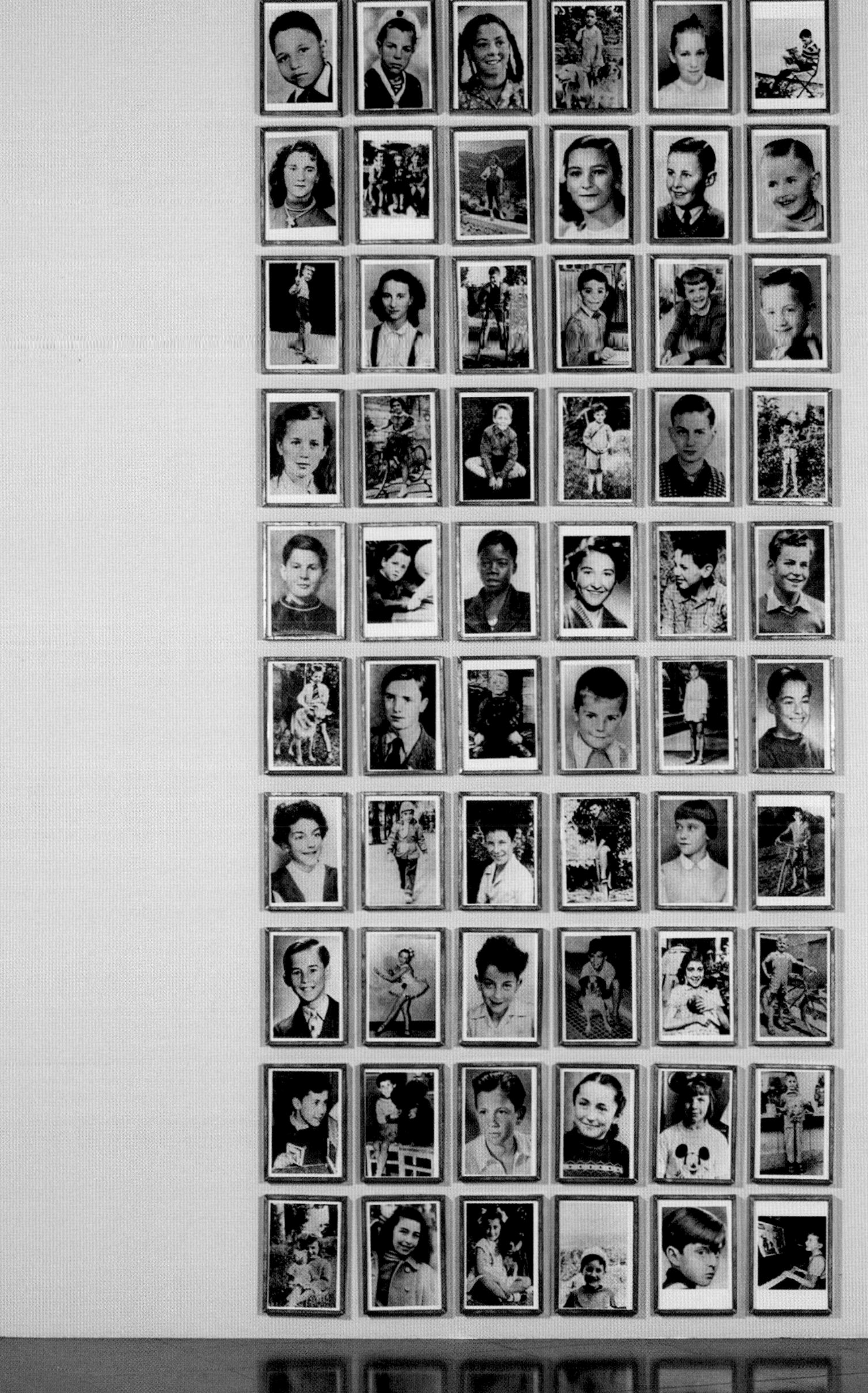

On Kawara (1932-2014) is a Japanese conceptual artist. His artistic research is based on a rigorous, repetitive protocol that uses the grid as a cataloguing structure. His best-known pieces include such series as *Today* (commonly referred to as Date Paintings), or the trilogy *I Met, I Went,* and *I Got Up*. The Date Paintings, for example, are monochrome canvases onto which the artist inscribes the day's date in white, in the language and script of the country where he is. Date Paintings stem from a daily ritual whereby the canvas is destroyed if not completed by midnight. The paintings also come with hand-made cardboard boxes that often contain a piece of newspaper showing the date itself. Like other series, this represents a sort of collection of reality coupled with the punctuation of the passing of time, without focusing on any one of these moments.

In 1955, before turning to Conceptual Art, Kawara produced a series of figurative drawings published at the time under the title *Death Masks*. Overlooked for decades, this series was released by the artist in 1995 under the name *Thanatophanies* and is today considered a pivotal step in our understanding of his continuing relationship with death. Kawara not only asserted his presence in the world through his Date Paintings, but also regularly sent telegrams to friends and acquaintances to let them know that he was still alive.

Thanatophanies, from Greek meaning "apparitions of death", is a series of thirty portraits inspired by actual press images or imaginative pictures of the victims of the Hiroshima and Nagasaki nuclear bombings. While Kawara never discussed these events directly, some of the photographic features and sources, and the details of the characters' ulcerations, suggest an association with the tragedy. Arranged in the form of a grid, the series raises the question of the subjects' identity. Are they portraits of the victims, or are they images taken elsewhere? We understand that these images "should not be understood as representations of 'specific' people", but instead as portraits of a sample of society. The original drawing lends a nightmarish dimension by placing the heads against a misty background. Here, the grid allows us to perceive in a single glance the versatility of these portraits and their deformations, including disturbing smiles and fragments of faces that beg the question as to their true nature. Death masks, of course, but of a death that is not only that of the physical body but also that of a daily life that consumes us day after day. Radiation acts as a metaphor for a death that can be immediate or very slow, especially in the repercussions caused by the genetic mutations of future generations. With his collections of reality, Kawara confronts us with our very existence, and the *Thanatophanies* are now as topical as ever. **VP**

Bibliography

Braxton, Mycah, « 'A Weapon to Change Modern Reality': Action and Agitation in On Kawara's *Thanatophanies, 1955–1956* » October, 163, 2018, p. 102-130.

Duroux, Xavier and Gautherot, Franck (dir.), *On Kawara: whole and parts 1964-1995*, Dijon, Presses du réel, 1996.

Thanatophanies

1955-1995

Portfolio of 30 engravings,
30 x (43 x 33 cm)
M HUKA / Vlaamse Gemeenschap Collection, inv. BK009083, Antwerp
© One Million Years Foundation 2023

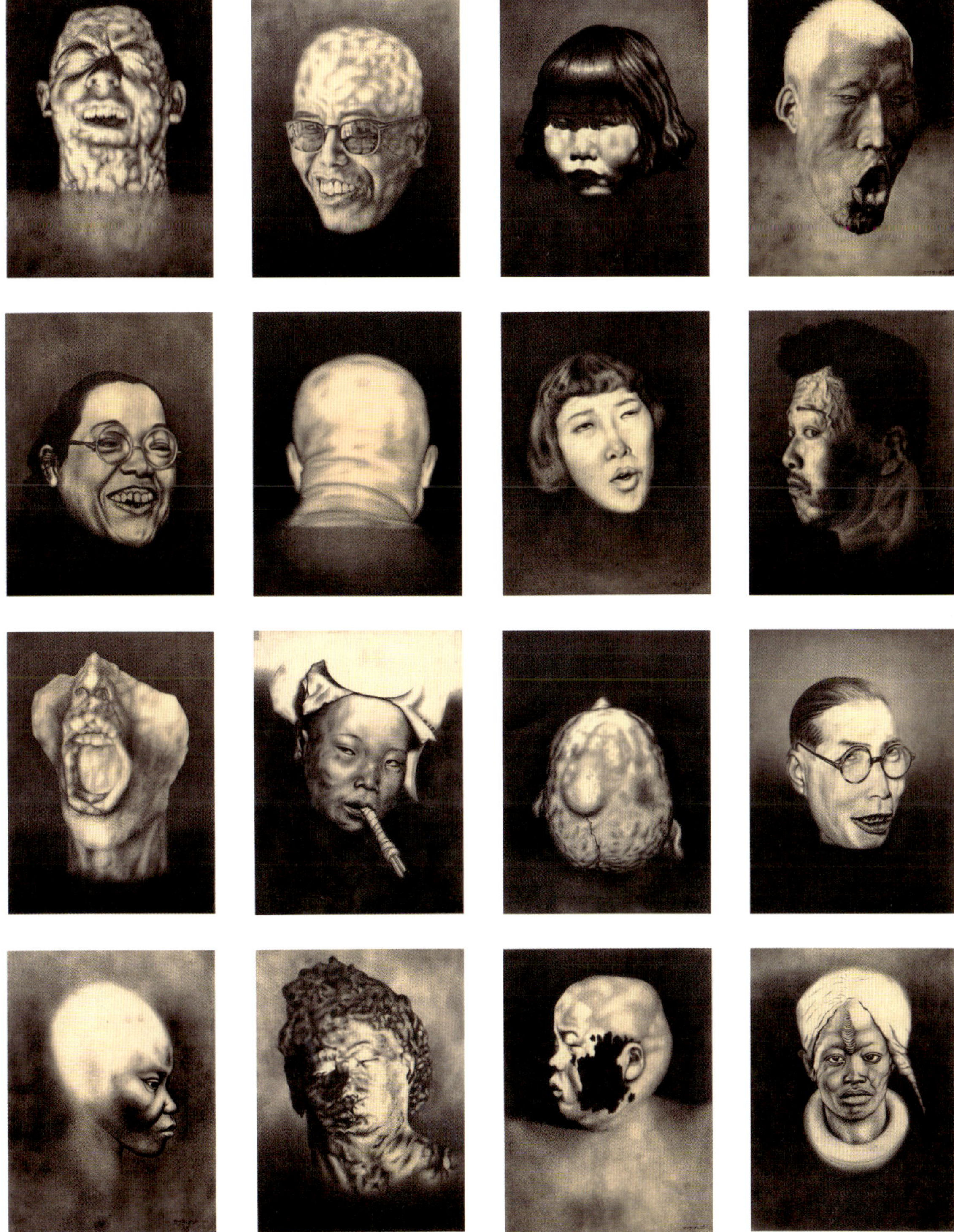

Claudia Andujar, born in Neuchâtel in 1931, is Swiss by birth. In 1944, she left Europe to flee the persecution of the Nazi regime. After immigrating to the United States, she moved to Brazil in 1955. In 1971, she was introduced for the first time to the Yanomami, an indigenous people living in the Amazon region. This encounter was to have a lasting impact on both her personal life and her artistic practice. From this point onwards, Andujar began defining the very specific outlines of her photographic practice, combining anthropological immersion, activist documentary work, and the subjective recording of the cosmovision and daily life of these indigenous people. During the 1970s and 1980s, Andujar visited the Yanomami on several different occasions and recorded the violence to which they were exposed, mainly under the development policy of the military dictatorship (1964-1985). Indeed, several villages were displaced to allow for the construction of major motorways such as the Trans-Amazonian highway in 1972. The growing community of miners in the region also spread "white man's" diseases to the more isolated groups.

In 1978, Andujar started to campaign more actively for the demarcation of Yanomami territories, and, between 1981 and 1984, she took part in humanitarian missions and vaccination campaigns. The *Marcados* series was produced in this context. In contrast to the artist's other dreamlike and poetic photographs, the intention here is to inventory individuals who were already immunised. Since they could not reveal their names in this context, they were photographed wearing small, numbered plates around their neck, which were subsequently appended to the medical files. On this occasion, the artist employed some of the representational conventions of anthropometric and forensic photography: the frontal view of the subjects, close framing centred on the faces, their isolation against a relatively neutral background and the inclusion of an identifying number.

In light of Andujar's past, this system is reminiscent of the concentration camps' markers such as the yellow star and digital tattoos. When Andujar revisits the negatives of these photographs and shows them as a work of art, she reveals the potentially problematic dimension and the "ambiguous feeling that

Claudia Andujar

*Horizontal e Vertical (Ericó, RR),
Marcados series, 1983*

has led me, sixty years later, to transform the simple record of the Yanomami as 'people' – branded to live – into a work that questions the method of labelling people for whatever ends. I now see this work, an objective effort to organize and identify a population at risk of extinction, as something on the verge of a conceptual piece."

From 2005 onwards, the portraits in this series have been shown in a variety of formats and arrangements, such as *Horizontal e Vertical (Ericó, RR)*, consisting of an enlarged portrait and a composition of thirty-six photographs reminiscent of a contact sheet featuring several snapshots arranged in strips to form a miniature grid. The decision to extract a portrait from the mesh of individuals and enlarge it underlines the expressiveness and singular identity of the subject, which cannot be reduced to the number inventorying it. **OA**

Bibliography

ANDUJAR, Claudia, *Claudia Andujar: Marcados*, São Paulo 2009.

NOGUERIA, Thyago (dir.), *Claudia Andujar : no lugar do outro*, cat. (July-November 2015), São Paulo, Instituto Moreira Salles, 2015.

Horizontal e Vertical
(Ericó, RR),
Marcados series
1983

Ink with mineral pigments on Hahnemühle
Photo Rag Baryta 315g paper,
30 × 35 cm and 57 × 38.5 cm
© Claudia Andujar 2023.
Courtesy Galeria Vermelho et
Piet Van Cauwenberghe & Anne De Man

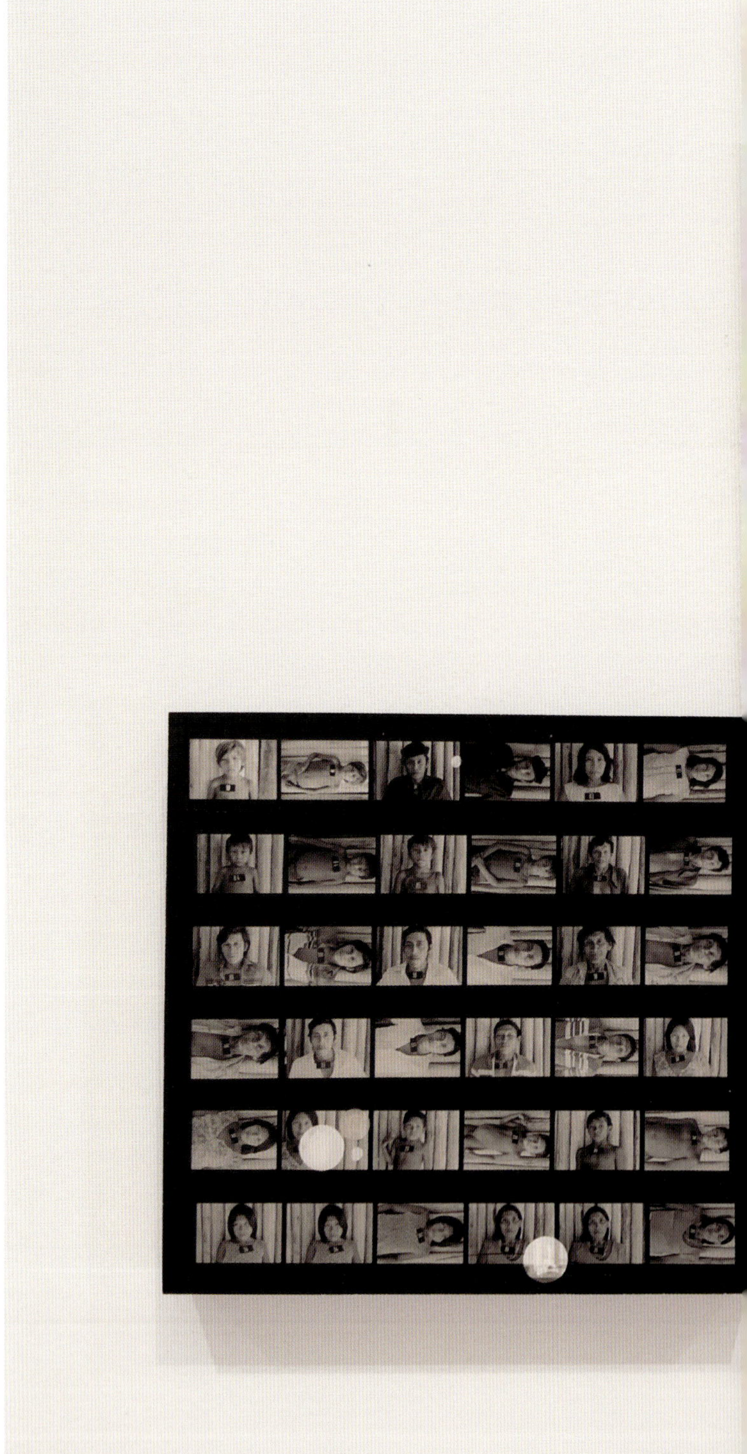

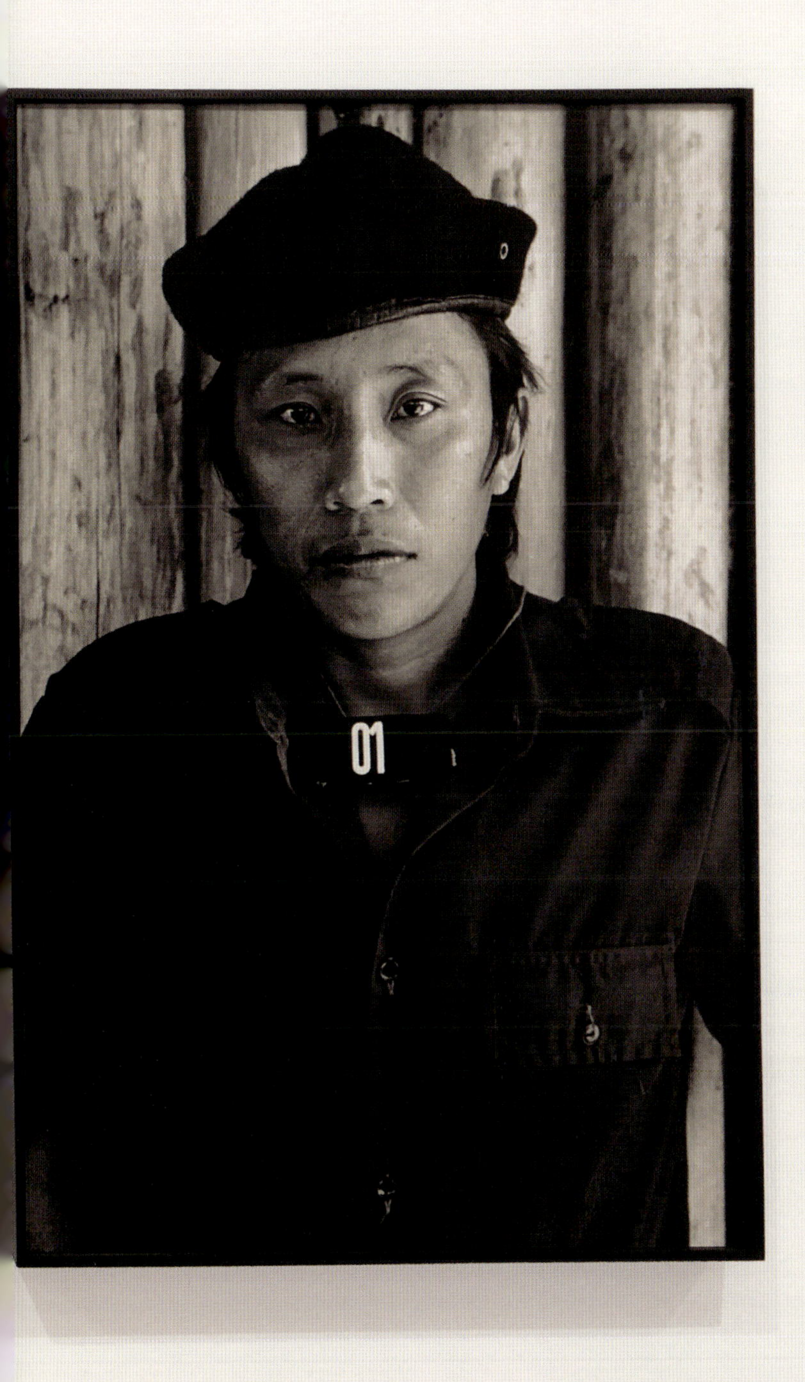

Michael Ensdorf is an American artist and professor of photography. He graduated from Columbia College in 1986 with a Bachelor of Arts in Photography and from the University of Illinois at Chicago in 1990 with a Master of Fine Arts. He is the founder of the Gage Gallery, which is affiliated with Roosevelt University where he teaches. He regularly uses the grid as a presentation device in his photographic work. This is particularly true for *Fiction* and *Minor Players*, two projects that paved the way for *Memory Grid*.

As part of the 1992 exhibition at the Detroit Artist Market Gallery, Ensdorf presented these two interlocking pieces in the form of a grid symbolising the falsification of memory induced in images produced by the media. While *Fiction* is based on historical images edited to reflect the artist's distancing from the events depicted, *Minor Players* focuses on the anonymous witnesses to these historic events by enlarging, within the space of a grid, their faces captured in the background of the photographs.

Ensdorf's reflection on the falsification of memory and his use of anonymous faces inspired his *Memory Grid*. This piece assembles several deformed anonymous faces in the shape of a grid. The photos are drawn from digitised media images, advertisements, and family snapshots, which are then decomposed and reconstructed using Photoshop. The images were then entered into the software, cropped, and enlarged. Then, pixels were added to the images through a process of interpolation, rendering them unrecognisable. Lastly, the colour of the images has been saturated to lend them a monochrome aspect. Through this process, Ensdorf explores photographic vision by tackling the information that triggers our memory when we observe a photograph. A photograph is a source of reminiscence, but it can also distort memory by being instantaneous and incomplete. The images presented in *Memory Grid* are unrecognisable and non-individual, enabling everyone to read what they want into them. Thus, the artist is assessing the extent to which he can take his image-modification process forward, while preserving the element that triggers the reminiscence. Ensdorf has adopted this line of research precisely because

Michael Ensdorf
Memory Grid, 1995

identity, in the era of new technologies and modified images, has become an unstable, fluid notion. His conclusion would thus be this *Memory Grid*, which proposes an "inventory of possibilities", a database from which viewers will necessarily be able to find the face that will take them back to a certain event in their memory.

For this purpose, the grid layout is ideal. First of all, it alludes to the presentation of images in a digital database. Secondly, as Rosalind Krauss explained in her article "Grids", this pattern is conducive to infinite expansion and provides an opportunity to increase the database. Thirdly, a grid has the intrinsic quality of equalising its constituents and presenting them individually within a group. Each image is thus visible for what it is, without being dominated by the one alongside or by an attention-grabbing motif. In an email exchange with Michael Ensdorf, the artist rightly stated that "the *Memory Grid* acts against this tendency to place, categorise and label. The grid attempts to equalise faces and events, re-categorise, re-label and ultimately re-place the original image." **ED**

Bibliography

IGLHAUT, Stefan, RÖTZER, Florian, CASSEL, Alexis, VON AMELUNXEN, Hubertus and SCHNEIDER Nikolaus, *Photography After Photography: Memory and Representation in the Digital Age*, London, G + B Arts, 1997.

Memory Grid

1995

Laser print of digitised photographs retouched on computer,
variable dimensions
© Michael Ensdorf 2023

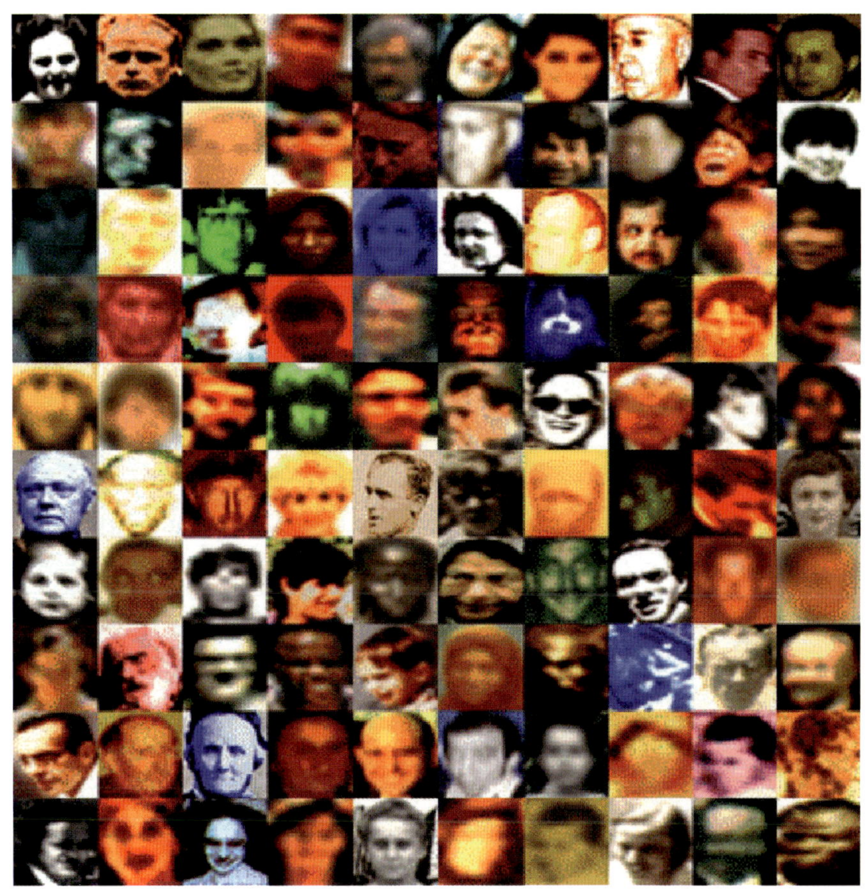

This book is published to mark the exhibition *The Grid. Trame. Grille. Matrice* on display between 6 October 2023 to 11 February 2024 at the Musée L – Musée universitaire de Louvain.

EXHIBITION

Exhibition curator
Alexander Streitberger

Exhibition production
Anne Colla, project coordinator

Direction a.i., Musée L
Elisa de Jacquier de Rosée

Exhibition and Publishing Department, Musée L
Anne Colla, Gwenaël Thomas,
Laurence Waterkeyn

Visitor Relations and Reception, Musée L
Marie Baland, Pauline Baltieri,
Flore d'Ansembourg, Sylvie De Dryver,
Stéphanie Delmotte, Terence François,
Manon Janssens, Isabelle Maron,
Joëlle Pigeolet

Collections Department, Musée L
Muriel Damien, Laura Debry,
Bénédicte Duvernay, Mickaël Lefèvre,
Laura Swalué, Marie Van Bosterhaut

Graphic design, Musée L
Joëlle Deuse

Administrative Department, Musée L
Anaïs Kasa-Vubu, Sophie Tumelaire

Loaners
CNAP, Espace de l'art concret, FRAC Franche-Comté, Grand Large (HDF), Lorraine, Normandie Caen, Occitanie Toulouse, Fédération Wallonie-Bruxelles, MAC's Grand-Hornu, Musée de la Photographie de Charleroi, M HKA, SMAK, ING Belgian Collection, Vanmoerkerke Collection, Philosophy Library of UCLouvain, Library of the Université Saint-Louis Bruxelles, KBR, Musée Wittert ULiège, Nadja Vilenne Gallery, Anita Beckers Gallery, Mendes Wood DM gallery, Mr Piet Van Cauwenberghe, Mr Bernd Stiegler, Mr and Mrs Guillaume Wunsch, Mr Michael Ensdorf

CATALOGUE

Publishing director
Alexander Streitberger

Texts by
Alexander Streitberger
Olivia Ardui
Elisa de Jacquier de Rosée
Célia Arias y Soto
Eléa Declercq
Valentina Perazzini

Editorial coordination
Laurence Waterkeyn (Musée L) and
Michelle Poskin (Éditions Racine)

Translation
Paula Cook

Graphic design
[nor] production – Emmanuel Bonaffini

Production and publishing
Éditions Racine, Brussels (www.racine.be)
Éditions Racine is part of the Lannoo
Publishing Group (www.lannoo.com).

Credits
The publisher has made every effort to contact the owners of the rights to the illustrations in this book. In the event that any photographs or illustrations were used without the knowledge of the copyright holders, please contact the Musée L. All rights reserved. No part of this publication may be reproduced, stored in a retrieval system, or transmitted in any form or by any means, electronic, mechanical, photocopying, recording or otherwise, without the prior permission of the copyright owner.

© 2023; L – UCLouvain Museum, the authors,
Uitgeverij Lannoo

D. 2023. 6852. 22
Legal deposit: October 2023
ISBN 978-2-39025-253-5

Printed in the European Union

Cover:
Vera Molnár, *100 carrés jaunes*
(Computer Icône 3), 1977
FRAC Normandie Caen Collection,
inv. FBN 1997-08
© Sabam Belgium 2023.
Photo François Fernandez

ACKNOWLEDGEMENTS

The Musée L would like to express its sincere gratitude to the following lenders, without whom this exhibition would not have been possible: the CNAP and the Espace de l'art concret, the FRAC Franche-Comté, Grand Large (HDF), Lorraine, Normandie Caen, Occitanie Toulouse, the Fédération Wallonie-Bruxelles, the MAC's Grand-Hornu, the Musée de la Photographie de Charleroi, the M HKA, the SMAK, the ING Belgian Collection, the Vanmoerkerke Collection, the Philosophy Library of UCLouvain, the Library of the Université Saint-Louis Bruxelles, the KBR, the Wittert ULiège museum, the Nadja Vilenne Gallery, the Anita Beckers Gallery, the Mendes Wood DM gallery, Mr Piet Van Cauwenberghe, Mr Bernd Stiegler, Mr and Mrs Guillaume Wunsch, Mr Michael Ensdorf.

We also salute the artists and their representatives for their support:
Claudia Andujar, Galeria Vermelho, Piet Van Cauwenberghe and Anne De Man
Eleanor Antin, Richard Saltoun Londres and Ronald Feldman Gallery New York
Henriette Coray Loewensberg
Analívia Cordeiro
Esther Ferrer
Anna Bella Geiger and Mendes Wood DM
Instituto Moreira Salles
Sherrie Levine and Xavier Hufkens
Marian Goodman Gallery
Manfred Mohr
Museo Reina Sofía
One Million Years Foundation
Rosana Paulino and Mendes Wood DM
Amy Plumb Oppenheim and Dennis Oppenheim Estate
Adriana Varejão
Guillaume Wunsch and Monique Van Kerckhove

We would like to extend our warmest thanks to the contributors and authors of this catalogue: Alexander Streitberger and Olivia Ardui for their essays; Elisa de Jacquier de Rosée, Musée L Director a.i., for her foreword; Célia Arias y Soto, Eléa Declercq, Valentina Perazzini for their research and writing.

And finally, we would also like to express our appreciation to all the students of the seminar "History of Art from the Avant-Garde to Contemporary Art" (UCLouvain) for their involvement in the project: Célia Arias y Soto, Charlotte Davister, Eléa Declercq, Juliette Droesbeke, Marguerite Glesner, Camille Guastaferri, Alice Merlin, Valentina Perazzini, Laura Weber.

With the support of

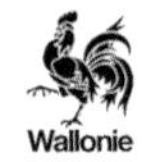 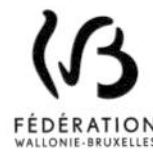 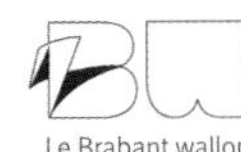 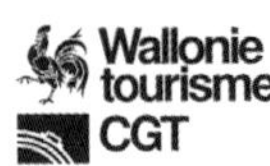 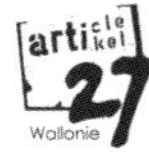

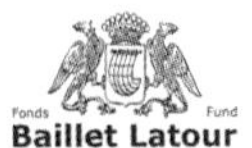 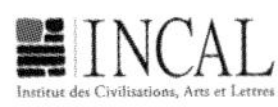 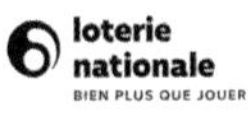 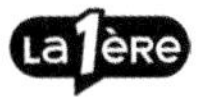 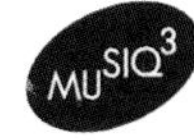

 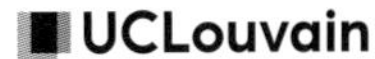

Musée L – Musée universitaire de Louvain
Place des Sciences 3 – 1348 Louvain-la-Neuve, Belgium